Abortion in a Crowded World

Also by S. Chandrasekhar

INFANT MORTALITY, POPULATION GROWTH AND FAMILY PLANNING IN INDIA
INDIA'S POPULATION: FACTS, PROBLEMS AND POLICY
ASIA'S POPULATION PROBLEMS (edited)
PROBLEMS IN ECONOMIC DEVELOPMENT (edited)
AMERICAN AID AND INDIA'S ECONOMIC DEVELOPMENT
RED CHINA: AN ASIAN VIEW
REPORT ON A SURVEY OF ATTITUDES OF MARRIED COUPLES TOWARD FAMILY PLANNING IN THE CITY OF MADRAS
COMMUNIST CHINA TODAY
A DECADE OF MAO'S CHINA (edited)
CHINA'S POPULATION: CENSUS AND VITAL STATISTICS
A REPORT ON SOUTH INDIAN READING HABITS
INFANT MORTALITY IN INDIA, 1901–1951
INDIANS IN SOUTH AFRICA: A SURVEY
POPULATION AND PLANNED PARENTHOOD IN INDIA
HUNGRY PEOPLE AND EMPTY LANDS
INDIA'S POPULATION: FACT AND POLICY
CENSUS AND STATISTICS IN INDIA
INDIAN EMIGRATION TO AMERICA
INDIA AND THE WAR

Abortion in a Crowded World
The problem of abortion with
special reference to India

S. Chandrasekhar

London   George Allen & Unwin Ltd
Ruskin House   Museum Street

First published in 1974

This book is copyright under the Berne Convention. All rights are reserved. Apart from any fair dealing for the purpose of private study, research, criticism or review, as permitted under the Copyright Act, 1956, no part of this publication may be reproduced, stored in a retrieval system, or transmitted, in any form or by any means, electronic, electrical, chemical, mechanical, optical, photocopying recording or otherwise, without the prior permission of the copyright owner. Enquiries should be addressed to the publishers.

© George Allen & Unwin Ltd 1974

ISBN 0 04 301066 0

This edition is not for sale in the USA or the Philippine Islands, where the book is published by the University of Washington Press, Seattle, Washington.

HQ766.5
.I5 C43
1974

Printed in Great Britain,
10/11 pt Times New Roman 327,
by W & J Mackay Limited,
Chatham

To the political leaders and medical scientists of the Soviet Union, who as early as 1920 pioneered in legalizing abortion

Preface

This volume owes its origin to an invitation to deliver the John Danz Lectures at the University of Washington, Seattle, in 1971. Three lectures on India's population growth and the liberalization of abortion law as a partial contribution to the solution were delivered extempore. But as there is no single study on the subject of abortion in India, I have enlarged the scope of the lectures by adding to what was orally delivered some material on the legislative process in India as well as some recent demographic data.

My grateful thanks for the honour of being appointed the 1971 John Danz Lecturer are due to President Charles E. Odegaard and Dean Joseph L. McCarthy of the University of Washington.

For his kind Foreword I am indebted to Professor Garrett Hardin of the University of California at Santa Barbara whose incisive and thoughtful writings on the subject of abortion are noteworthy.

My thanks are also due to the Editors of *The New York Times Magazine*, *Population Review*, *Foreign Affairs* and *Scientific American* for permission to use material contributed to their columns.

Lastly I would like to express my gratitude to all those authors, editors and publishers who have given me permission to quote from their books and articles. Footnotes at appropriate places indicate the sources.

La Jolla, California
15 December 1972

S. Chandrasekhar

The John Danz Lectures

In October 1961, Mr John Danz, a Seattle pioneer, and his wife, Jessie Danz, made a substantial gift to the University of Washington to establish a perpetual fund to provide income to be used to bring to the University of Washington each year '... distinguished scholars of national and international reputation who have concerned themselves with the impact of science and philosophy on man's perception of a rational universe'. The fund established by Mr and Mrs Danz is now known as the John Danz Fund, and the scholars brought to the University under its provisions are known as John Danz Lecturers or Professors.

Mr Danz wisely left to the Board of Regents of the University of Washington the identification of the special fields in science, philosophy, and other disciplines in which lectureships may be established. His major concern and interest were that the fund would enable the University of Washington to bring to the campus some of the truly great scholars and thinkers of the world.

Mr Danz authorized the Regents to expend a portion of the income from the fund to purchase special collections of books, documents, and other scholarly materials needed to reinforce the effectiveness of the extraordinary lectureships and professorships. The terms of the gift also provided for the publication and dissemination, when this seems appropriate, of the lectures given by the John Danz Lecturers.

Through this book, therefore, another John Danz Lecturer speaks to the people and scholars of the world, as he has spoken to his audiences at the University of Washington and in the Pacific Northwest community.

Foreword

For many years those of us in the Western world who are interested in population problems have been beholden to S. Chandrasekhar for insight into the fascinating problems of the largest nation for which we have firm demographic knowledge. His years of experience as a Member of Parliament and Minister of Health and Family Planning in the Government of India have given him an intimate knowledge and authority which few demographers have. The basic population problems may be said to be universal, but custom creates many special variants. By the comparative study of these variants we can hope to arrive closer to those truths we need to know to make possible man's survival in dignity. We can be grateful to Chandrasekhar for his clear exposition of the Indian scene, which he wisely correlates with a discussion of similar problems elsewhere in the world. A worthwhile book.

University of California, Santa Barbara   Garrett Hardin

Contents

Preface	*page* 11
Foreword	15

1 The Indian and the World View of Abortion — 21
Introduction	21
The Evolution of Religious Views on Abortion	25
The Soviet Union and the Socialist Countries	49
Great Britain and the Commonwealth	50
The New Climate in the United States	53
The Incidence of Abortion	54
Methods of Abortion	56
Abortion in India	59
The Pre-1971 Indian Law on Abortion	66

2 India's Population Problem — 68
Introduction	68
India's Population Growth: 1871–1971	69
The Problem	74
How India is Tackling her High Birth Rate	75
Areas of Ignorance	79
Conclusion	80

3 India Liberalizes her Abortion Law — 82
The Changing Climate	82
The Abortion Study Committee and its Recommendations	83
The Central Family Planning Council's Recommendations	86
History of the Current Liberal Legislation	88
The Abortion Bill as Introduced in the Rajya Sabha on 17 November 1969	90
The Reaction of the State and Union Territories' Governments to the Proposed Legislation	93
The Joint Select Committee's Report	100
Demographic Effects of Abortion	109
Conclusion	115

Appendixes
1 The Legal Status of Abortion in Selected Countries 1971	119
2 List of Diseases which are Medical Indications for Artificial Interruption of Pregnancy	120
3 Questionnaire of the Committee to Study the Question of the Legalization of Abortion	128

CONTENTS

    4 An Anonymous Report of Illegal Abortions done in an Indian Clinic *page* 134
    5 The Population of India according to the 1951, 1961 and 1971 Censuses   144
    6 The Religious Composition of India's Population according to the 1951, 1961 and 1971 Censuses   145
    7 Select Editorial Comment on Abortion from the Indian Press   146
    8 The United States Supreme Court Decision on Abortion   161

Glossary   168

Select Bibliography   171

Index   180

Tables

1	Foetal Deaths by Mothers' Age, 1955–1959	*page* 61
2	Incidence of Natural and Induced Abortions etc. 1960–1963	62
3	Growth of India's Population, 1871–1971	69
4	Possible Birth and Death Rates which may Account for Decennial Growth Rates	73
5	Numbers and Rates of Pregnancies, Abortions and Births in Japan, 1947–1957	111
6	Sterilizations in Japan, 1949–1956	113
7	Numbers and Rates of Pregnancies, Abortions and Births in Hungary, 1956–1966	115

Chapter 1

The Indian and the World View of Abortion

INTRODUCTION

What is an abortion?
The term 'abortion', in both legal and obstetric parlance, is generally applied to the premature expulsion of the product of conception, that is before twenty-eight weeks of pregnancy (the period after which the foetus is considered viable). An expulsion of the foetus at and after twenty-eight weeks and before the end of gestation is termed a premature birth.

But the term 'abortion', being both old and vague, has acquired in popular parlance a pejorative connotation. According to the dictionary, to 'abort' is to 'bring forth premature offspring' or to 'give birth prematurely'; but an 'abortionist' is 'a producer of illegal abortions'. Obviously one cannot call a surgeon who performs a legal abortion an abortionist. In the clinical sense abortion means the physiological process of evacuating a pregnant uterus, but in the legal sense it normally refers to induced abortion. Therefore the World Health Organization has attempted to standardize the meaning of the term in vital statistics by recommending 'foetal deaths' to cover all outcomes of pregnancy other than live birth and by further classifying foetal death as early, middle or late on the basis of the length of life from conception.

Abortions may be either spontaneous or induced. And induced abortions are divided into legal and illegal.

A spontaneous abortion is one that occurs naturally as a result of certain pathological conditions often beyond the control of the pregnant woman and the physician. In fact, a certain amount of pregnancy wastage occurs even before a woman is aware that conception has taken place, so that it is difficult to establish the incidence of spontaneous abortion. According to one estimate, there is about one spontaneous abortion for every five full term deliveries.

An induced abortion is the deliberate interruption of pregnancy by artificially inducing the loss of the foetus. The legality of an induced abortion depends on the particular laws in force in a country. In some countries only a therapeutic abortion, carried out to save the life of the mother, is legal. In some other countries an induced abortion may be permitted not only to safeguard the mother's physical and mental health but also on humanitarian, demographic, economic, eugenic and social grounds. Of late, abortion laws which were rigid and strict in many countries during the first half of this century have been gradually liberalized. In some countries the picture is rapidly changing.

Man, through the ages from primitive, non-literate societies to advanced, industrialized and sophisticated societies, has attempted to control conception by a variety of largely crude and rule-of-thumb methods. When he failed to prevent conception he tried to interrupt pregnancy. When this did not succeed certain societies even resorted to infanticide.

Perhaps the earliest recorded contraceptive prescriptions are those found in early Egyptian Kahun Papyrus dating back to about 1850 BC. The Ebers Papyrus of 1550 BC, considered 'the most ancient book in the world', contains what is believed to be the first reference in writing to a prescription to prevent conception.[1]

As for abortion, (that is induced abortion, meaning human interference with and termination of an unwanted pregnancy within a particular period), it has been resorted to by almost all societies, at different periods of history, for a variety of reasons. These have been cases of incest, rape, pregnancy in an unmarried girl, pregnancy in a girl below the age of consent, and pregnancy in a sick or emotionally disturbed woman. Abortion has also been carried out to ensure the physical health or sheer survival of a woman. Besides these considerations, abortions have been carried out when a pregnancy showed lack of spacing, when it has occurred during the lactation period, or for certain eugenic reasons.[2]

But although abortion was and is widely practised, nearly all cultures and societies have tried to control and regulate it, whether through social *mores*, moral conventions, religious taboos or government laws and regulations. The codes of some of the earliest civilizations that arose in western and southern Asia – centuries before the Christian era – dealt with it and reflect the concern of the community with the problem, which is as old as attempts at contraception, if not considerably older.

The Sumerian Code of 2000 BC, the Assyrian Code of 1500 BC, the Hammurabic Code of 1300 BC, the Hindu Code of about 1200 BC and the Persian Code of 600 BC—all dealt with the problem of induced abortion. They prohibit and punish such acts as striking an expectant

---

[1] Norman E. Himes, *Medical History of Contraception* (New York, Schocken Books, 1970), p. 63.
[2] George Devereaux, *A Study of Abortion in Primitive Societies* (New York, the Julian Press, 1955), *passim*.

mother or indulging in any act that leads to the loss of an unborn infant. The laws of the day tried not only to protect the pregnant woman but also to compensate her for the loss of her unborn child.

The Jewish people described in the Old Testament (*circa* 600 BC) knew of various birth control methods. The withdrawal method – coitus interruptus or onanism[3] – was certainly known, though it is difficult to estimate how widespread the practice was.

As for abortion, the Old Testament refers briefly to accidental miscarriage, and does not specifically touch on induced abortion, for possibly it was not a serious problem among the Jews then. The relevant passage in Exodus reads:

If when men come to blows, they hurt a woman who is pregnant and she suffers a miscarriage, though she does not die of it, the man responsible must pay the compensation demanded of him by the woman's master; he shall hand it over after arbitration. But should she die, you shall give life for life, eye for eye, tooth for tooth, hand for hand, foot for foot, burn for burn, wound for wound, stroke for stroke.[4]

The Talmud, on the other hand, which contains only one reference to abortion, appears to be more humane and lenient on the question.

If a woman is in hard travail [and her life cannot otherwise be saved], one cuts up the child within her womb, and extracts it member by member, because her life comes before that of [the child]. But if the great part [or the head] was delivered, one may not touch it, for one may not set aside one person's life for the sake of another.[5]

In other words, the foetus can be sacrificed to save the life of the mother, and this stand is more rational than that of Exodus.

There are references in the Hindu *Upanishads* (*circa* 1500 BC) to certain methods of controlling conception. The *Brihadyogatarangini* contains several contraceptive recipes including a method for the occlusion of the cervix. It is possible that this later work took this material from Charaka's medical writings, which according to

---

[3] 'There Judah saw the daughter of a certain Canaanite whose name was Shua; he married her and went in to her, and she conceived and bore a son, and he called his name Er. Again she conceived and bore a son and she called his name Onan. Yet again she bore a son and she called his name Shelah. And Judah took a wife for Er his firstborn, and her name was Tamar. But Er, Judah's firstborn, was wicked in the sight of the Lord; and the Lord slew him. Then Judah said to Onan, "Go in to your brother's wife, and perform the duty of a brother-in-law to her and raise up offspring for your brother." But Onan knew that the offspring would not be his; so when he went in to his brother's wife he spilled the semen on the ground, lest he should give offspring to his brother. And what he did was displeasing to the sight of the Lord, and He slew him also.' Genesis 38: 2–10.
[4] Exodus 21:22–5.
[5] Talmud, Tohoroton II, oboloth 7:6.

one writer can be assigned to the first century BC. But more of the Hindu view later.

About the seventh century AD certain Chinese medical texts (as in Sun Ssu-mo's book *Chien Chin Fang*) offer several contraceptive methods.

As for abortion, it is probable that its practice in its crudest form, as already pointed out, is as old as man. Certainly all civilizations for which we have any records at all show that abortions have been in vogue for thousands of years. In fact, it is possible that abortion might well have been the first kind of 'surgery' ever attempted by man. Devereux, who has carefully examined all societies for which any documentation is available at all, is convinced that abortion is an absolutely universal phenomenon.[6]

Man's attitudes toward abortion have ranged over a wide spectrum, from approval, bordering on encouragement, to total prohibition and condemnation; all the way from the early civilizations—Assyrian, Babylonian, Hindu, Greek and Roman, to the present day.

Most of the Greek philosophers, particularly Plato and Aristotle, approved of it and even encouraged it. Plato (*c*. 427–348 BC) in his *Republic* examines almost everything under the sun including such modern problems as communism, democracy, women's liberation, birth control, abortion and eugenics. To Plato, 'a child's education should begin before birth', meaning he must be born of select and healthy ancestry. Therefore only healthy men and women should have children and hence the need of a health certificate for every bride and groom. Men may reproduce only when they are over thirty and under forty-five; women only when they are over twenty and under forty. Offspring born of unlicensed matings, or deformed, are to be exposed and left to die. Before and after the ages specified for procreation, mating is to be free, on condition that the pregnancy be aborted.

We grant this permission with strict orders to the parties to do all in their power to prevent any embryo from seeing the light, and if any should force its way to birth, they must understand that the offspring of such a union cannot be maintained, and they must make their arrangements accordingly ... Our model community would, of course, be pacific, for it would restrict population within the means of subsistence ....[7]

Aristotle (384–322 BC) was equally permissive. According to him, 'If it should happen among married people that a woman, who already had the prescribed number of children, became pregnant,

[6] George Devereux, *A Study of Abortion in Primitive Societies* (New York, Julian Press, 1955), *passim*.
[7] *The Republic*, 5,461C; Will Durant, *The Story of Philosophy* (New York, Simon & Schuster, 1961), p. 31.

then before she felt life, the child should be driven from her.' He was also of the view that any woman who conceived after her fortieth year should have an abortion. As Durant summarizes:

> The state should determine the minimum and maximum ages of marriage for each sex, the best seasons for conception, and the rate of increase in population. If the natural rate of increase is too high the cruel practice of infanticide may be replaced by abortion and 'let abortion be procured before sense and life have begun'.... There is an ideal number of population for every state, varying with its position and resources.[8]

THE EVOLUTION OF RELIGIOUS VIEWS ON ABORTION

THE EARLY CHRISTIANS

The attitude of the early Christian Church towards sex, marriage and family was largely derived from Judaism, which viewed women as inferior persons but as the important source of children. The commandment in the Book of Genesis was clear: 'Be fruitful and multiply, and replenish the earth, and subdue it; and have dominion over the fish of the sea, and over the fowl of the air, and over every living thing that moveth upon the earth.' Apart from this commandment, the Jews believed that the continuance of the family and racial line and the preservation of the Jewish way of life, that of a 'chosen people', were of paramount consideration. Hence the importance of the need for large numbers.

The first four hundred years of the Christian era constituted a difficult and demanding period for the Christians. Contemporary historical circumstances shaped their attitudes, behaviour and doctrine. They were surrounded by a pagan world which not only persecuted them for their beliefs, but practised a different standard of sexual morals leading to a denial of the sanctity of marriage and of the worth and dignity of human life. And medical knowledge was barely a few steps beyond superstition. The continuance, indeed the survival, of the Christian community after persistent martyrdom was of crucial importance. Hence to the Christians anything that interrupted human life, be it contraceptive potion or poison or abortion, was disapproved of and denounced as murder.

An intellectual product of these times was St Augustine (354–430). With a guilty conscience stemming from years of immoral life before his conversion, he defined a simple but rigid Christian attitude to sexual morals. To begin with, current views held that worldly life was evil and sex was sinful. The Pauline slur on sex was, however, con-

---

[8] *Politics* VII, ch. 16; Will Durant, op. cit., p. 67.

doned with the injunction 'Better marry than burn'. And to St Augustine the next step was simple enough. Sexual intercourse within marriage without procreation was a sin. And this view set the pattern and influenced succeeding generations of Christian theologians and commentators for almost a thousand years.

Nine centuries after Augustine, St Thomas Aquinas (1225–74), the Italian theologian, corroborated and expanded Augustinian morals with the dictum that anything that interfered with procreation was a sin against nature. Aquinas became to the Catholic Church what Vatsyayana was to Hindu ethics, even prescribing the righteous and sinful postures in coitus. The influence of Aquinas was so compelling that the Catholic doctrine on contraception and abortion became rigid, irrational and cast-iron. There were countless subtle, hair-splitting variations of the theme with succeeding generations, but the basic ban on birth control became widespread in the Western Christian world and continues in the Catholic world almost to this day.[9]

Thus these Catholic views became the foundation for various laws on the matter in Europe in the eighteenth and nineteenth centuries. For instance, in France, incredible as it may sound, a 1939 law stipulates the guillotine as a punishment for abortion; nor was it one of those laws that are honoured more in its breach than otherwise, for in 1942 a woman abortionist was actually sent to the guillotine! And possibly the greatest incidence of abortion, and the consequent high death rate because of it, are to be found in such backward 'Christian' countries as Spain and Portugal, where the laws are most medieval and where, even today, abortion is not legally permitted for any reason whatsoever.

THE CATHOLIC VIEW

The Catholic Church, alone among all the great religions, through many centuries of acrimonious comment and controversy, has always taken the stand of absolute prohibition of abortion. Many volumes have been written on the Catholic view not only of birth control in general, but of abortion as well. There is no need to explore these well-known views beyond a brief summary and a short evaluation of their relevance in the present-day world.

The Roman Catholic Church, which claims nearly 615 million members – though it is unnecessary to add that all do not strictly follow its directives – holds even today that a new life (ensoulment? or is it later at quickening?) begins at conception, and therefore the

[9] For an excellent review of early Christian thought on the subject see John T. Noonan, Jr, *Contraception: A History of its Treatment by the Catholic Theologians and Canonists* (Cambridge, Harvard University Press, 1965), pp. 137–211.

removal of a zygote, embryo or foetus is considered a murder and is hence forbidden. The only possible exception is in the case of indirect abortion, when an operation is performed to cure a fatal disease of the mother which incidentally leads to the destruction of a foetus. Thus an ectopic pregnancy or a cancerous pregnant uterus may be removed as these operations have the primary purpose of saving the life of the mother, not the destruction of the foetus, which is secondary.

This interpretation of the Catholic teaching, despite centuries of biologically meaningless controversy, is however, of recent origin. It is based on canon 2350 of Pope Benedict XV in 1917, and on the encyclical *Casti Connubi* (*Christian Marriage*) issued by Pope Pius XII in 1930.

The Catholic case against abortion cannot be expressed better than in the words of Pope Pius XII:

The unborn child is a human being in the same degree and by the same title as its mother. Moreover, every human being, even the child in its mother's womb, receives its right to life directly from God, not from its parents, nor from any human society or authority.... Innocent human life, in whatsoever condition it is found, is immune, from the very first moment of its existence, to any direct deliberate attack.... The life of an innocent human being is inviolable, and any direct assault or aggression on it violates one of those fundamental laws without which it is impossible for human beings to live safely in society.

In short, the encyclical *Casti Connubi* summarizes the Church's ban against abortion as follows: 'The life of each [mother and foetus] is equally sacred and no one has the power, not even the public authority, to destroy it.' This encyclical also reaffirms the Catholic Church's traditional ban against all contraception (barring the rhythm or safe period method), as it involves a deliberate 'limitation of the generation of offspring', which is 'an act against nature'.

More recently, Pope Paul VI, in his encyclical *Humanae Vitae* (*The Value of Human Life*), issued in 1968, points out: 'We must once again declare that the direct interruption of the generative process already begun, and above all directly willed and procured abortion, even if for therapeutic reasons, are to be absolutely excluded, as licit means of regulating birth.'

The present writer had an audience with His Holiness the Pope at the Vatican in 1967 and explained India's governmental and voluntary efforts to promote planned parenthood, which include all birth control methods. But the Pope, after expressing great concern for India's overpopulation problem, opposed both voluntary sterilization (vasectomy and tubectomy) and induced abortion or anything that interferes with 'the genesis of life', as he put it, even for the Hindus and other non-Catholics in India and elsewhere. I pointed out to the Pope that his attitude was not dissimilar to that of some Hindu religious leaders who are strict vegetarians, who believe in *Ahimsa* (non-cruelty to all living things), and who would like to crusade against the killing of animals for human consumption by all Christian and other non-vegetarians.

When Does Life Begin?

Two issues arising from the Catholic Church's absolute ban on abortion need clarification.

First, when the Church contends that abortion is 'wilful destruction of life', it is not clear what is meant by 'life'. Apart from other factors, the crux of the problem rests on the definition of this term. Most biologists would agree that the term 'life' is arbitrary in the context of both the origin of life on the planet and the origin of an individual's life. And yet the question of when life exactly begins has not yet received an adequate and scientific answer, though the philosophies of all major religions have their own theories.

Does life begin when the egg is released? For after all the egg's 'intent' is to meet the sperm, and 'intent' is important in all theological discussions. Or does life begin when the cells are undergoing meiosis? Or when the egg is fertilized and becomes a zygote?—it has the potentiality, if everything goes well for the next nine months, of a future infant. Or does life begin when the fertilized ovum is implanted in the wall of the womb (nidation) and begins to develop into an embryo?—because normally a woman cannot have an abortion until implantation has taken place.

The contention that life is created only when the sperm fertilizes the ovum somehow implies the somewhat unbiological view, in the deeper sense, that the ovum and spermatozoa are not alive, or at least that they are only half alive entities, and life is created only when these two 'lifeless' entities meet. Maybe the gamete has only half a soul!

Some cultures believe that the egg is life. Certainly no one can seriously deny that life exists in the egg and the sperm long before they are mature and are released. Many Hindus, and particularly the Jains, do not consume eggs because that would be destroying life. Therefore, to some, life's beginning can go back to a stage before conception. If this is accepted, nature is the most awful killer for wasting, as she does, the billions of sperm that do not penetrate ova, not to speak of all the ova that are wasted on the women of the world who do not become pregnant. If one is serious about the real genesis of life, one should go back, far back to the primordial beginning. This need not be dismissed as mere Hindu theological casuistry.

As Dr George W. Corner, the distinguished American embryologist, points out,

Is the unfertilized egg a living thing? In one sense, no. It cannot reproduce itself unaided, nor even maintain itself more than a day or two. In another sense, yes, for its biochemical make-up contains substances necessary for life and produced only by living organisms—in this case by the mother when it is formed in the ovary. But its store of such substances must be augmented by the sperm cell if it is to survive and develop. It is as much alive as a new-laid unfertilized hen's egg, or as the ovule in the female flower of an oak tree, and no more. If indeed we may properly use the word 'life', for which there is no satisfactory definition, we might say that the human egg cell briefly possesses half a life.[10]

What about the embryo? Professor Garrett Hardin compares the early embryo with a set of blueprints. It contains specifications for a new human being and if it is lost or removed it can be repeated many times. Therefore, while the embryo has life potential as much as the sperm or the egg, it is not the same as a live-born infant or an adult human being. His observations are worth quoting at some length:

When does a human life begin? Molecular biology has given us new insights into the nature of life, individuality, and reproduction—insights that have important implications for the ethical problem of the value of life. . . . In biology, the meaning of the word 'life' has been successively redefined. . . . At first we saw life as an ethereal substance passed on from parent to offspring (or from divinity to new human being). The concept of 'soul' seems to be a substantial one (at least it was initially). Later, as it became clear that the death of an organism resulted in no substantial loss, recourse was had to new ideas related to energy. . . . The greatest progress in understanding the puzzle of 'life' has come as we have turned our attention from substance and energy to the new concept of information. What distinguishes a living from a non-living thing is not peculiar substances or new forms of energy, but unique organization; but the rapid progress we have made in the last few decades makes it quite clear that there is nothing like it in the non-living world.

Organization is essential to life. The act of reproduction is basically one

[10] George W. Corner, 'An Embryologist's View', in Robert E. Hall (ed.) *Abortion in a Changing World* (New York, Columbia University Press, 1970), pp. 3–4. In an earlier work Dr Corner points out: 'The embryologist is keenly aware – who could know it better? – that the egg is endowed with the marvellous gift of life, but he sees this as a general property of organic creatures and he would never have conceived the idea that an immaterial self-conscious existence, destined to endless bliss in heaven or the torments of the pit, is entrusted to the uncertain custody of the human egg.' (*Ourselves Unborn: An Embryologist's Essay on Man* (New Haven, Yale University Press, 1944), pp. 120–1.

in which the information specifying the organization is replicated and the products separated into different packages, which we call 'individuals' (individual cells or individual organisms). By far the greater part of the information is contained in the nucleus of the cell, specifically in the chromosomes, and even more specifically, in the deoxyribonucleic acid (DNA) of the chromosomes.

DNA is like a tape with five billion spots of information. It is the sequence of these spots in the DNA of a zygote that determines whether a man or a monkey will be produced, and if it is a man, whether he will have light hair or dark, erythrocytes that are sickle cells or normal, whether saccharine will taste sweet or bitter to him, and whether or not his urine will smell unpleasant after he eats asparagus.

With no serious qualifications we can say that all the information needed to produce an adult is found in the tiny amount of DNA enclosed in the nucleus of the zygote. Tiny? Yes, indeed! The weight of the DNA of one fertilized egg is only 6 picograms. To use a homely comparison, the amount of zygote DNA needed to specify *all* of the world's population of 3·5 billion people weighs only one-seventeenth as much as one postage stamp. This is microminiaturization of information with a vengeance....

With these facts as a background, let us look once more at the moral problem of abortion. Again it will help if we introduce an analogy. Consider the case of a man who is about to begin to build a fifty thousand dollar house. As he stands on the site looking at the blueprints a practical joker comes along and sets fire to them. The question is: can the owner go to court and collect fifty thousand dollars for his blueprints? The answer is obvious: since another set can be produced for the cost of only a few dollars, that is all they are worth. (A court might award a bit more for the loss of the owner's time, but that is a minor matter.) The moral: a non-unique copy of information that specifies a valuable structure is itself almost valueless.

The principle is precisely applicable to the moral problem of abortion: the zygote, which contains the complete specification of a valuable human being, is not a human being and is almost valueless. The work of Gertig, Rock and Adams has revealed that at least 38 per cent of all zygotes produced are spontaneously aborted. What is the loss? Very nearly zero, even when the zygotes have reached the foetus stage. Actually the aborted foetuses are mostly defective, so there is truly a human gain; but even if they were not defective, the human loss would be negligible. The early stages of an individual foetus have had very little human effort invested in them; they are of very little worth. The loss occasioned by an abortion is independent of whether the abortion is spontaneous or induced. (Just as the loss incurred by the burning of the blueprints is independent of whether the causal agent is lightning or an arsonist.)

A set of blueprints is not a house; the DNA of a zygote is not a human being. The analogy is deficient in only two respects, which are interesting rather than important. The blueprints of the zygote are constantly replicated and incorporated in every cell of the human body. But there is no moral obligation to conserve DNA—if there were, no man would be allowed to brush his teeth and gums, for in this brutal operation hundreds of sets of DNA are destroyed daily.[11]

When then does life begin? Life does not begin or emerge at a fixed point; it is a continuous and dynamic process. While a cycle has no beginning, and paradoxical as it may seem, the cycle of life may be taken to begin with the creation of sperm and ova, which join to make a new being, who in turn may reach puberty and create sperms or ova, and the cycle goes on endlessly. Dr Malcolm Potts sums up the position admirably:

There is no single event marking the beginning of life, there is no Rubicon to be crossed during embryological development upon which we can concentrate and say, 'Before this moment we have an object as trivial as a nail-paring; after this time we have an individual human being to which we must reserve the full sanctity of human life.' An ethical system founded on biology must begin by recognizing that reproduction is a continuum which can be traced back to the time when the primordial germ cells are first recognizable in the yolk sac endoderm (at about the twentieth day after fertilization in man) and it is still incomplete when a grandmother baby-sits for her daughter's children. During this long process fertilization is an incident which is biologically important but so remote from the interests of society that the woman in whose body it occurs has no way of knowing what has happened.[12]

Professor Glanville Williams, the British jurist, after examining the relevant legal and moral evidence, points out:

There is a third possible line in the prenatal period which might be established by the legislature as the beginning of legal protection. This is the time of viability, conveniently fixed at the twenty-eighth week of pregnancy. It may well be that, as a political matter, a radical reform of the present abortion law could best be achieved by fixing this time as the datum. Whatever social arguments may be used, many people will continue to regard abortion as abhorrent because of the sanctity of the young life that is destroyed. That there is weight in this view cannot be denied. The humane, ethical, and parental feeling of the plain man leads him to wish to extend the protection of the criminal law not only to the newly born child but to the viable child before birth. The protection need not, however, be extended beyond viability. As Lord Riddell pointed out, 'the destruction of a full-grown child is a revolting affair, whereas the abortion of an early foetus differs but little from the removal of a uterine tumor.'

A line drawn at the twenty-eighth week would be socially satisfactory because illegal abortions do not take place after this time: in fact, few occur after the first four months of pregnancy.

[11] Garrett Hardin, 'Blueprints, DNA, and Abortion: A Scientific and Ethical Analysis', *Medical Opinion and Review* (February 1967).
[12] Malcolm Potts, 'The Problem of Abortion', in F. J. Ebling (Ed.), *Biology and Ethics* (London and New York, Academic Press, 1969), pp. 74–5.

In between the time of quickening and the time of viability one might take the time at which the foetal brain begins to function. The soul, after all, is frequently associated with the mind and until the brain is formed there can be no mind. By placing electrodes on the maternal abdomen over the foetal head, electric potentials (brain waves) are discernible in the seventh month, that is shortly before the time of viability. If one were to compromise by taking, say, the beginning of the seventh month as the beginning of legal protection for the foetus, it would practically eliminate the present social problem of abortion.[13]

It is therefore doubtful if there is any modern biological opinion that supports any one theory on when life begins to the exclusion of others. Perhaps the answer is not that science has failed, but that the question is considered not meaningful. Perhaps some philosophy might offer an answer where science has not come up with a definitive one.

The Hindu philosophers posed this question centuries before the Christian canonists came on the scene. According to the Hindu classical texts there are three schools of thought: (1) that life begins with conception, (2) that it begins with the first movement of the foetus, and (3) that it begins with the first breath of the infant after delivery, just as it ends with the last breath.[14]

According to the Hindu view, life or the breath of life – *prana* – is simply a series of births. Life is both the beginning and the end. In other words, life is both birthless and deathless, without beginning, without end, eternal and everlasting. The egg, the sperm, the blastocyst, the zygote, the embryo, the foetus and the infant—all are life, one stage more developed and valuable than the earlier. But the *atman* (soul) is not the conscious self till it has seen the light of day. And further, with growth to adulthood, there are different levels of life, each different from the other, depending upon the depth of physical maturity, intellectual awareness, and spiritual perception. But in another and *karmic* sense of predestination, death is also life, for it ushers one into the 'next world' of which we know nothing.[15] That is, to those for whom the cycle of births has ended there can be no rebirth; the individual soul (*atman*) becomes merged into the cosmic soul (the Brahman). But to millions in this life there may not be an unknown other world because they may be reborn immediately into another life, higher or lower, depending upon the kind and

[13] Glanville Williams, *The Sanctity of Life and the Criminal Law*, third printing (New York, Knopf, 1968), pp. 230–2.
[14] S. Radhakrishnan, *The Hindu View of Life* (London, Allen & Unwin, 1955), *passim*; also his *Principal Upanishads* (London, Allen & Unwin, 1953).
[15] *The Katha Upanishad* says: 'The Knowing Self is not born; It does not die. It has not sprung from anything; nothing has sprung from It. Birthless, eternal, everlasting and ancient It is not killed when the body is killed.' (I. ii. 18)

quality of life led in the present birth. Thus death is only the genesis of life. But this is Hindu philosophy and not biology.

One more question. At what stage of biological development – ovum to an adult who is able to produce more ova – is a human being a person, full and fulfilled? But this fruitless quest can go on endlessly.

Philosophical speculations apart, it is a biological fact that at least one in about three fertilized eggs or embryos fails to develop correctly and dies in the uterus, resulting in spontaneous abortion or reabsorption. It is estimated that about half of the foetal wastage occurs before the fourth or fifth week. Does this spontaneous abortion – Nature's 'balance' or God's own work, if you will – constitute destruction of life? One wonders.

But to millions who are faced with the agonizing abortion dilemma, granting that induced abortion is 'destruction of life'; the best that can be said is that it is a matter of choice between two evils. When the choice is forced, the lesser evil is preferred. One may have to exchange the life of the zygote, embryo or the unborn foetus for the fuller life of its mother because on her life depends in many ways the life of other children, the life of her husband and other members of the family, and the larger family – our society – that has invested in her growth, education and development.

The Sanctity of Life

Apart from the question of when life begins, the second issue is the Catholic concern about the 'sanctity of life'. Undoubtedly any crusade against violence, murder and war is welcome in this violent and wartorn world. And no wonder all great religions and ethical systems put great value on the sanctity of life. But is the 'sanctity of life' an unqualified one?

This plea for non-violence would sound admirable had the Catholic Church been against all wars, which destroy at the very least the flower of the youth of the warring sides. This is what may be called absolute pacifism. But the Catholic Church has never taken an uncompromising stand against killing *adult* human beings as the Quakers,[16] Gandhians[17] and other pacifists have done. Had the teachings and actions of the Catholic Church through the centuries been singularly pacifist, and had it taken (or took now) an absolute stand against the destruction of any human life, no matter what the

[16] For a progressive pacifist point of view see the report prepared by the American Friends (Quakers) Service Committee: *Who Shall Live? Man's Control over Birth and Death* (New York, Hill & Wang, 1970).
[17] For detailed views of Mahatma Gandhi see D. G. Tendulkar, *Mahatma: Life of Mohandas Karamchand Gandhi* (Bombay, Jhaveri & Tendulkar, 1952), 8 vols.

reason, then one could perhaps appreciate its abhorrence of taking the life of a fertilized ovum. But on the contrary, the Catholic Church and its proponents, if one understands the history of the Catholic Church correctly, have indulged in countless bloody and miserable killings for reasons that have seldom been profound, even granting for a moment that any war can really have a profound cause. In view of this, the Catholic Church's concern for the sanctity of life and the life of the unborn sounds extremely hollow, as by any reckoning its concern for human life over the centuries has been ambiguous at best. One thinks not only of the Crusades and the Inquisition, but of a myriad other miseries that the Catholic Church has forced on humanity in the name of God, Christ and Religion.[18]

It is true that most, if not all, religions have wielded the sword while preaching peace. But the Christian Church has been particularly notorious in this direction, not only waging religious wars against other denominations and converting harmless 'heathens' but also conducting imperialist wars, subjugating peoples and plundering colonies. The Christian Church, alone among the religions, offers the extraordinary spectacle of bishops blessing bombs and battleships but opposing birth control and abortion, all in the name of the Prince of Peace. No heathen world could ever have coined the slogan 'Praise the Lord and pass the ammunition'. There is apparently some logic in this absurdity, for if mass massacre should be justified, the sources that provide the fodder for periodic slaughter should not be permitted to dry up.

If one really believes in the sanctity of life one should go to the logical lengths of Hinduism, Buddhism and Jainism with their *Ahimsa* (non-violence or non-injury to all life), which holds that it is evil knowingly to destroy any living creature. Sanctity of life includes the entire animal kingdom, with the Jains going so far as to wear a surgical mask lest they breath in and destroy the tiny insects in the atmosphere. By the same token one should shelter rats and roaches, snakes and vermin, for after all, they are living creatures.

However, the Catholic Church has never been bothered about the ethics of the abattoir. Schopenhauer remarks that when an animal

[18] Dr S. Radhakrishnan, former President of India and a distinguished philosopher, writes, 'In 1929, after the concordat between Mussolini and the Holy See, the Pope saluted the Italian Fascist dictator Il Duce as a "man of God" and in 1932 he gave him the Papal blessing at St Peter's. Four years later, the Italian clergy were ordered to celebrate the Fascist victory over Ethiopia with special services for thanksgiving in the churches. In the same year (1936) in the Spanish Civil War, the Pope anathematized the Republican forces as satanic and blessed the armies of General Franco, who decorated his guns with the emblem of the Sacred Heart of Jesus!' (S. Radhakrishnan, *Recovery of Faith* (New York, Harpers, 1955), pp. 27–8.)

devours another the pleasure of the eater is never so great as the pain of the one being eaten. And vegetarian George Bernard Shaw hoped that his hearse would be followed by flocks of sheep and herds of cattle and a menagerie of live fish all mourning the man who would rather die than eat his fellow creatures. Eating one's fellow creatures is not exactly the best way to promote the concept of the sanctity of life. But Catholic theologians have never shown any interest in the moral claims of vegetarianism. One might reply that it is not fair to imply that the believer in the sanctity of *human* life need not logically believe in the sanctity of *all* life. But the point here is that just as a non-vegetarian discriminates between different forms of life, one should logically differentiate between different stages of prenatal life—from the fertilized ovum to the 9-month-old foetus.[19]

Two more rather minor objections have been raised against abortion. One is that the embryo, though within the womb, is a separate individual entity. It is contended that abortion is not so much a medical and humanistic problem of unwanted pregnancy as the raising of an ethical and philosophical question of 'whether pregnancy is a relationship between two human beings, one dwelling within the other'. The answer is that a normal pregnancy, when the child is wanted, is a joyous affair, but we are considering the unwanted pregnancy, unwanted for a variety of valid reasons. So long as the foetus is organically a part of the mother and receives support and sustenance from the overall maternal physiological system, the embryo has no individual identity of thought and communication and no independent viable existence. Its removal for certain good reasons cannot be treated as very different from amputation. The severing of a sick limb to enable the larger and more important body to survive is not only not murder: it is really a renewal of life, which otherwise may be threatened. As the *Bhagavad-Gītā* puts it, an evil averted must be greater than the evil committed.

The other contention is that 'from the union of germ cells there is under normal development a living, definitely going concern. To interrupt a pregnancy at any stage is like cutting the link of a chain; the chain is broken no matter where the link is cut'. There are two ways of meeting this contention. First, it is, of course, true, but the problem is that it is not always a question of 'normal development'. And even when physical development is normal, there are abnormal, socio-economic and psychological considerations which rob the pregnancy of its normal character. Secondly, a moment's reflection will show that strict adherence to this dogma would sanction

[19] Dr Albert Schweitzer, in discussing his principle of reverence for life, once remarked with a smile, 'But you see, I am not consistent; I decline meat, yet I am very fond of eggs'.

euthanasia of post-reproductive persons, since they are, biologically, not part of the 'chain'.

In a sense, it is true that the interruption of a pregnancy is like cutting the link of a chain. A link may be cut but many new links can be forged easily. As it is true that the chain is broken no matter where the link is cut, does not the relatively tremendous, and natural and spontaneous wastage of sperm and eggs and fertilized ova constitute a serious severance of the chain? In the biological cycle starting with the egg and ending with the adult producing eggs, the loss of an egg or ovum or a zygote is as much an interruption as the removal of an embryo. In reply to this, the Catholic Church would probably say 'yes', but our response is that it is something we can do nothing about, whereas we can do something about induced abortions.

In brief, the entire Catholic theological position on human reproduction is that nothing should be done to control, manage or regulate it, with the possible exception of the 'safe period' method which has proved quite unsafe to countless women. The Church's laudable desire to promote virtue and discourage sin has compelled it to ignore the economic, demographic, eugenic, humanitarian, social and pathological factors that perennially surround human life. To the Church, the traditional virtues have always seemed to be more important than poverty, misery, disease, war and death. How else can one equate the denial of procreation within marriage as equivalent to converting the bridal chamber into a brothel. To the Church the pursuit of a self-imposed traditional virtue is so spiritual that the world[20] can cheerfully bear population pressure and all its attendant miseries. There should be no place for such sickly sentimentalism in a rational world.

Catholic theology appears to be changeless and monolithic. Scientific truths constantly change as new discoveries render former truths obsolete, and the admission of past errors becomes easy. But

[20] In defence of the Catholic Church it must be pointed out that it is apparently not in quest of more souls for the Catholic faith. Mere self-interest should make the Church happy that non-Catholics practise contraception and reduce their numbers. It is, therefore, a measure of their strong belief in this matter that they oppose abortion in Hindu India, Muslim Pakistan or Turkey or a Buddhist or Shinto Japan. But why worry about the pagans whose lot after death the Church is so clear about? This selfless stand in not opposing the proliferation of non-Catholics is difficult to understand. One wonders.

On the other hand, in 1959 the Catholic Truth Society of London in a pamphlet addressed to British Catholic wives put the matter in a different light: 'Our faithful Catholic mothers are doing a wonderful work for God. In time, if contraceptive practices continue to prevail amongst Protestants, their number will decrease and the Catholic race will prevail, and thus England might again become what it once was, a Catholic country.' (*A Talk to Catholic Wives* by a Catholic woman doctor (London, Catholic Truth Society, 1959), p. 26.)

because theology professes eternal truths, dogmas in general persist through the ages. There is no point in changing beliefs based on ignorance because evidence becomes irrelevant. But even Catholic theology sometimes changes long after the truth has been established, and long after even the faithful have ceased to care. Galileo was made to recant his belief that the earth moves around the sun but no one bothers today about the Church's flat earth mentality.

Unfortunately when the Catholic Church does change its attitude no one can undo the incredible cruelty and misery that have already been imposed on the helpless faithful. How can one estimate the enormous hardship that women have been forced to endure through the ages by man's unyielding interpretation of the divine will? While it is astonishing that the bigotry of an ignorant minority can hold up the progress of the great majority of mankind, courageous dissent and thoughtful independence even among the faithful have not always been wanting. As a Catholic writer reviewing the Church's position on contraception and related questions puts it,

When primitive man was trying to press northward from the tropics and was worrying how his naked body would stand the winter cold, it is fortunate he had no witch-doctors (the Catholic Church) to limit him to three choices: (1) Don't go north (complete abstinence); (2) Go north only in the summer time (periodic abstinence); or (3) Go north as you are and trust in the spirits of your clan (accept all the biological consequences of your action). But man found a fourth choice, 'instant fur', and became thereby the most adaptable mammal.[21]

As the Catholic Church and its adherents look back on these times a quarter or half a century from now, their descendants are likely to marvel at the foolish wickedness of their ancestors.

THE PROTESTANT VIEW

It is true that till the first quarter of the twentieth century all the Protestant denominations, like the Church of Rome, were hostile to the idea of contraception and abortion on the grounds that they were immoral, unchristian and contrary to divine law.

The Lambeth Conference of 1920 warned against

the use of unnatural means for the avoidance of conception, together with the grave dangers – physical, moral and religious – thereby incurred, and against the evils with which the extention of such use threatens the race. In opposition to the teaching which, under the name of science and religion, encourages married people in the deliberate cultivation of sexual union as

[21] Julian Pleasants, 'The Lessons of Biology', in Thomas D. Roberts (ed.), *Contraception and Holiness – the Catholic Predicament* (New York, Herder & Herder, 1964), p. 92.

an end in itself, we steadfastly uphold what must always be regarded as the governing considerations of Christian marriage. One is the primary purpose for which marriage exists, namely the continuance of the race through the gift and heritage of children; the other is the paramount importance in married life of deliberate and thoughtful self-control.[22]

Ten years later, the Protestant interpretation of the divine will changed when the Lambeth Conference of 1930 approved contraception, although conditionally.

It is axiomatic that parenthood is for married people the foremost duty; to evade or disregard that duty must always be wrong. It is equally axiomatic that the state of marriage is a divinely ordained relationship in which intercourse between men and women calls for the highest exercise of the Christian virtues of self-discipline, self-control and self-sacrifice. . . . It follows, therefore, that it can never be right to make pleasure or self-indulgence the motive for determining to limit or refuse parenthood. Equally, it can never be right for intercourse to take place which might lead to conception where a birth would involve a grave danger to the health, even to the life, of the mother, or would inflict upon the child to be born a life of suffering; or where the mother would be prematurely exhausted, and additional children would render her incapable of carrying out her duties to the existing family. . . . It will be admitted by all that there are circumstances in married life which justify, and even demand, the limitation of the family by some means.[23]

Twenty-eight years later the approval of contraception became unanimous. The Lambeth Conference of 1958 approved it in terms of the following resolution:

The Conference believes that the responsibility for deciding upon the number and frequency of children has been laid by God upon the consciences of parents everywhere: that this planning, in such ways as are mutually acceptable to husband and wife in Christian conscience, is a right and important factor in Christian family life and should be the result of positive choice before God. Such responsible parenthood, built on obedience to all the duties of marriage, requires a wise stewardship of the resources and abilities of the family as well as a thoughtful consideration of the varying population needs and problems of society and the claims of future generations.[24]

In addition, the Conference went one step further and approved abortion at the dictate of strict and undeniable medical necessity, broad enough to cover health as well as life.

[22] *The Lambeth Conference, 1867–1930* (London, 1948).
[23] *The Lambeth Conference 1930* (London, SPCK, 1931).
[24] *The Lambeth Conference, 1958* (London, 1958). For a discussion of the Protestant theological view of coitus *vis-à-vis* the concept of henosis see S. Chandrasekhar, *Population and Planned Parenthood in India* (London, Allen & Unwin, 1961), pp. 60–4.

Various Protestant denominations in the United States of America have approved not only contraception but also abortion in recent years. The National Council of Churches in 1961 approved hospital abortion 'when the health or life of the mother is at stake'. It stressed the sanctity of potential life and condemned abortion as a method of birth control.

The positions of individual Protestant denominations vary. Generally, abortion is tolerated when the health or life of the mother is threatened. Some denominational policy statements are given below.

The American Baptist Convention in 1968 recognized 'that abortion should be a matter of responsible personal decision' and urged legislation to provide that (1) the ending of a pregnancy before the twelfth week 'be at the request of the individual(s) concerned and be regarded as an elective medical procedure governed by the laws regulating medical practice and licensure'; and (2) after that period a pregnancy be terminated 'only by a duly licensed physician at the request of the individual(s) concerned' for reasons suggested by the Model Penal Code of the American Law Institute (substantial risk to physical or mental health of the mother; risk that the child would be born with grave physical or mental defect; rape, incest, or other felonious acts as the cause of the pregnancy).

The 1968 resolution continues: 'Further, we encourage our churches to provide sympathetic and realistic counselling on family planning and abortion. We commend study, research, and development of understanding on the part of the populace led by the people of our churches toward an enlightened view of this provocative problem.'

In October 1965 a committee of the Board for Social Responsibility of the Church of England declared:

... the problem of abortion is precisely the problem of weighing the claims of the mother against the claims of the foetus and vice versa, when they conflict, though it is important that neither be thought of in isolation from the family group of which they are a part.

... in certain circumstances abortion can be justified. This would be when, at the request of the mother and after the kind of consultation which we have envisaged (the pooling of the knowledge and judgements of the general practitioner, a psychiatric or other consultant, a medical social worker, a psychiatric social worker, or other person professionally interested in the case), it could be reasonably established that there was a threat to the mother's life or well-being, and hence inescapably to her health, if she were obliged to carry the child to term and give it birth. And our view is that, in reaching this conclusion, her life and well-being must be seen as integrally connected with the life and well being of her family.

[The] consultative procedure would cover those cases where justification for abortion would rest upon there being an assessable risk of a defective or deformed child, as well as cases of incest or rape, though the ground of the decision would be the prognosis concerning the mother as affected by the pregnancy in question; not the possibility of deformity itself, not simply the fact (if established) of the act of incest or of rape.... [The suggested consultation, in cases where abortion is not indicated] would give the patient access to the skilled medical and social services which can afford her the encouragement, help and support which she may need to continue the pregnancy and give birth to the child.[25]

According to the United Presbyterian Church (1962 General Assembly): 'One of the issues often discussed is the question of priority as to saving the mother's life or the child's life. This must be decided on the basis of the specific medical problems involved.'

The Unitarian Universalist Association (1968 General Assembly) urges 'that efforts be made to abolish existing abortion laws, except to prohibit performance of an abortion by a person who is not a duly licensed physician, leaving the decision as to an abortion to the doctor and his patient'.

Thus the Protestant Church unlike the Catholic Church, has, in response to man's changing needs and the threat of overpopulation approved not only contraception but abortion as well.

THE HINDU VIEW: THE SCRIPTURES

Whatever may be the fixed intellectual beliefs of other religions, there is no single, static, dogmatic, time-bound belief in Hinduism's attitudes to abortion and other problems of human life. The Hindu view of any aspect of life, be it birth or death, marriage or migration, is a composite summation of certain principles enunciated in classical Hindu scriptures, the various perceptive and learned commentaries – both of approval and disapproval – of later *Acharyas* (religious commentators) like Sankara (ninth century AD) and Ramanuja (eleventh century AD), centuries-old customs and traditions which came to have the force of law, secular laws promulgated by Hindu rulers and modern court rulings. Nevertheless, one can talk of a, if not the, Hindu view of a specific subject if the view is understood to be relevant to a particular historical period when the majority of Hindus held a certain belief or practised a particular way of life. Even in this restricted sense, exceptions have not been wanting, for there are differences between regions and sects.

The *Vedas* (*c.* 2000–800 BC), the earliest Hindu scriptures, are four in number: the *Rig-Veda*, *Sāma-Veda*, *Yajur-Veda* and *Atharva-Veda*. The fourth and last Veda, the *Atharva-Veda*, composed be-

[25] As quoted in *Who Shall Live? Man's Control over Birth and Death* (New York, Hill & Wang, 1970), pp. 97–8.

tween 1500 and 1000 BC, is the earliest available document on Indian medicine. It contains 731 hymns dealing with medical lore of the day, including charms and incantations, potions and spells.

Although there is actually no Veda called *Ayurveda*, Susruta, one of the founders of the Hindu system of medicine, gives the name *Ayurveda* to an *upanga* (sub- or supplementary Veda) of the *Atharva-Veda*. In later years, *Ayurveda* was elevated to the status of a Veda to give the system of medicine the necessary priestly authority and sanctity. The word *ayurveda* is derived from *ayuh*, which means life, and *veda*, which means knowing or attaining. Thus *ayurveda* is a system of knowledge that enables one to understand, protect and prolong human life.

The first reference to abortion is found in the Atharva-Veda. The passage opposing abortion reads: 'On Trita the gods wiped off this sin, Trita wiped it off on human beings; hence, if Grahi [attack of disease] has seized thee, make these gods remove her by means of their charm! Enter into the rays, into smoke, O sin; go into vapours and into the fog! Lose thyself on the foam of the river! Wipe off, O Pushan, the misdeeds on him that practiseth abortion.'[26]

The following explanation of the passage is offered by the translator. Trita was created as a scapegoat for the gods. But she did not carry the guilt that had been placed upon her; instead she unloaded it on someone else who, being already guilty, was a fit scapegoat. In later literature the story is elaborated with many variants, in each of which the details differ. Yet the general idea is that guilt is passed from one to another in an ascending order of wickedness. Pushan is a god of wayfaring, hence of those who are lost on their way.[27] Here he assumes a role derived from his function of protecting lost travellers: protecting sinners, for they have lost their way in life. He takes away disease which is a symbol of guilt, dissolves the guilt itself in vapour. But even a god has to put guilt somewhere, so he is asked to 'wipe it off' on the person who practises abortion. The roundabout implication is that abortion is a serious sin.[28]

Another passage in the Atharva-Veda condemns abortion because 'within the womb Prajapati is moving: he, though unseen, is born in sundry places. He with one half engendered all creation: what sign is there to tell us of the other?' Prajapati is, of course, the creator, the Lord of the Universe and fountainhead of all progeny.[29] This is

[26] 'Hymns of the Atharva-Veda' trans. M. Bloomfield, in F. Max Muller (ed.), *Sacred Books of the East* (Oxford, Clarendon Press, 1879–1910), XLII, 165.
[27] Alain Danielou, *Hindu Polytheism* (New York, Pantheon Books, 1964), pp. 123–4.
[28] See Germain Grisez, *Abortion: The Myths, the Realities and the Argument* (New York, Corpus Books, 1970), p. 119.
[29] Alain Danielou, op. cit., pp. 238–40.

another way of saying that abortion is inimical to the very elemental principle of creation.

Hindu scriptures apart, the Hindu lawgivers of a later age treated abortion as a crime and ranked it among other crimes such as murder, incest, adultery with the wife of a guru (teacher), etc. Manu (*c.* 200 BC), the major Hindu law-giver, dismissed abortion as a mere cause of impurity. According to him, libations shall not be offered to women who drink alcohol, live with many men, kill their husbands, have abortions, or join a heretical sect or cause.[30]

Hindu Medicine

Our knowledge of ancient Hindu medicine is derived from three Indian medical classics in Sanskrit. The first was written by Susruta, a physician, the second by Charaka, a surgeon, and the third by Vaghbata I, a medical compiler and annotator. There have been numerous other minor writers and commentators, noteworthy among them Nagarjuna, Bhava Misra, Madhavikara, Vaghbata II, etc.

The *Charaka Samhita*, which is ascribed to the period 58 BC to AD 123, deals with the 'science of life', bodily ailments and possible cures. He prescribes diet, medicines and a regimen which will restore harmony in life.

The second most important source of ancient Indian medicine is *Susruta Samhita*. This is the major, if not the only, source of ancient Hindu surgery, and is ascribed to the fifth century BC. Vaghbata I wrote a compendium of general medicine, *Astanga Samgraha* (Eight-part Collection), and this work is believed to belong to the period between the sixth and seventh centuries AD.

Charaka, Susruta and Vaghbata explore the subject of gynaecology and obstetrics at some length in their treatises. While the first writer confines himself to the medical aspects of gynaecology, Susruta deals with the surgical aspect of obstetrics. These works inquire into such subjects as the structure and function of male and female reproductive organs, puberty, menstruation, menopause, fertility, sterility, conception, development of the foetus, labour, abortion and miscarriage.

It is interesting to note that there is a discussion of various signs in pregnancy which supposedly indicate whether the foetus is male or female. In fact, directions on the most appropriate time for conception and other details to ensure that the child will be of the desired sex, are not wanting. Their discussion on abortion and miscarriage includes signs, symptoms and causes of abortion and treatment of incipient and threatened abortion, etc.

[30] 'Laws of Manu' trans. George Buhler, in F. Max Muller, op. cit., xxv, p. 184

According to Susruta,

> Any menstrual flow in the second and third months of pregnancy should be considered an abortion [*garbhasrava* or *garbha-vichyutih* or quasi-miscarriage]. This is presumably a spontaneous one. The foetus is in a liquid state for the first four months and hence its destruction or issue from the womb is called an abortion; the limbs of the foetus gain in firmness in the fifth and sixth months of pregnancy and its issue at this time is called *garbha-pata* [induced abortion].[31]

And as for the causes of abortion, Charaka writes:

> Excessive increase of the *doshas* (bodily humours), over-indulgence in food and drink of keen and 'heating' properties; suppression of the urgings of *vayu* (wind), urine and stools, indulgence of food made of 'hostile' ingredients; use of uneven beds and seats; pressure on the womb, wrath, grief, envy, malice, fear, and apprehension; other acts which bring about the premature destruction of the foetus are excessive sexual intercourse, emetics, venesection, purgatives and enemas up to the eighth month of pregnancy.[32]

(Charaka here, I believe is not making a clear distinction between induced and spontaneous abortions.)

Both Charaka and Susruta give directions on how to avoid an abortion.

> The pregnant woman should avoid all acts harmful to the uterus, such acts as a blow on the foetus, constant pressure on that part of the abdomen, travel in a bad conveyance on uneven roads, hearing of sudden loud sounds ... she should not sleep on her back, for the umbilical cord may twine round the neck of the foetus.[33]

According to the medical historian, Arturo Castiglioni,

> The formation of the embryo was the subject of long and accurate investigation in the Indian medical texts. The process of development and all the phenomena that occur in uterine life, especially those of the circulation, were studied. Main indications are given to distinguish various periods of pregnancy and no less detailed prognostic information on the influence of various phenomena on the foetus. A deep knowledge of applied physiology was considered to be necessary for the study of pathogenesis and pathology.[34]

The only relevant point to be made here is that these early writers were aware of some of the problems related to foetal growth and abortion. And what is astonishing is that their knowledge, judging

---

[31] *Susruta Samhita*, II:8, 9.
[32] *Charaka Samhita*, IV:8, 62.
[33] *Susruta Samhita*, III:8-10.
[34] Arturo Castiglioni, *A History of Medicine*, translated from the Italian and edited by E. B. Krumbhaar (New York, 1941).

from the period in which they wrote, is not more unscientific. Certainly they were no more ignorant, perhaps less ignorant, of these problems than their contemporaries in other parts of the world.

Induced Abortion

As for induced abortion, the Hindu scriptures from the Vedic age down to the *Smritis* (100 BC–AD 100) called it *bhruna-hatya* (foetus murder) or *garbha-hatya* (pregnancy destruction), and condemned it as a serious sin. According to *Vishnu Smriti* (*c.* 100 BC–AD 100), 'The destruction of an embryo is tantamount to killing a holy or learned person'. According to *Yagnavalkya Smriti* (*c.* AD 400), 'The undoubted degradation of women is caused by sexual intercourse with the lowly born, causing abortion [on oneself] and causing injury to the husband. Yagnavalkya repeats the same sentiments when he states that *garbhapatana* [being guilty of inducing abortion] is one of the valid reasons for abandoning one's wife.'

References to induced abortions are found in ancient Hindu texts from the *Rig-Veda*, the *Kathaka Samhita*, the *Taittreya Aranyaka* down to the *Dharma Sutras* and later *Smritis*. Some references to abortion are also found in the later epics, the *Mahābhārata* and the *Rāmāyana* (*c.* 500 BC–AD 500). The following reference in the *Mahābhārata* suggests the Hindu attitude of the period toward abortion: '... letting a woman's *Rtu* [fertile period] go to waste was a sin tantamount to embryo murder'.

That almost all ancient Hindu writers and law-givers refer to induced abortion and condemn it as a serious sin reveals the prevalence of induced abortion even then. Thus the problem has been with us for some four thousand years and more.

But as in all codes of ethics, there is in the Hindu view an admirable and practical dichotomy of the ideal and the permissible. The ideal code of behaviour was for the dedicated 'righteous' or saintly minority and the permissible way was for the work-a-day millions. Thus while the ancient Hindu law-givers condemned induced abortion severely, they did provide for difficult and exceptional cases.

Susruta, for example, was of the opinion that early pregnancy could be terminated if the pregnant woman's health were seriously affected. He advises: '[When the health of the pregnant woman is threatened and her condition becomes serious] the pregnancy may be terminated to save her life because it is improper to let the pregnant mother die. So the proper step is to induce abortion.'

This humane and wise counsel of the ancient Hindu may be contrasted with the conservative Catholic view of much later times. What is more, the Ayurvedic tradition progressed even further in later centuries, for Acharya Lolimbaraj, a well-known Ayurvedic physician who flourished in the seventeenth century, in his work *Vaidya Jeevanam* (*A Physician's Life* or *Medical Life*), says, 'If the root of the herb *Indrayam* is kept in the vagina, menstrual discharge begins. It is a useful remedy for pregnant women in poor health, widows and women of liberal morals'.

If classical Hinduism opposed abortion, twentieth-century Gandhian Hinduism did not have to take a stand on abortion for the country was not aware of the magnitude of the problem. Mahatma Gandhi was, of course, opposed to family planning in the sense of scientific contraception, since he was a firm believer in continence and moral restraint.[35] But Radhakrishnan, who has reinterpreted classical Hinduism in the light of modern thought and needs, has approved of contraception and would permit abortion under certain conditions.[36]

Thus the Hindu view has never been static. It has adjusted itself to altered world conditions and changed economic and social needs. The history of social legislation of free India – a secular India despite the large majority of Hindu population – reveals that in a conflict between modern scientific outlook and traditional religious attitude, the former has often won. The religious beliefs of a bygone age have been compromised in the face of pressing modern needs. That is how a preponderantly Hindu parliament could pass the abortion measure more easily than many a Western Christian nation.

THE MUSLIM VIEW

The Muslim attitude toward abortion is important, for the adherents of Islam today number more than 500 million and constitute the majority community in twenty-two countries including Indonesia, Pakistan, the United Arab Republic, Turkey, Iran, Malaysia, Morocco, Afghanistan and Algeria. And in certain other countries such as India, the Muslims constitute important minorities.

Despite partition and the creation of Pakistan and Bangla Desh, there are in India today more than 61 million Muslims, according to the 1971 census. They are India's largest minority and are Indians in every sense of the term, except that they profess a different religion from that of the majority community of Hindu Indians. Their welfare is of great concern to the Government and people of India.

Unfortunately no authoritative study of the demography of Indian Muslims has ever been made and no reliable information is available

[35] M. K. Gandhi, *Birth Control: The Right Way and the Wrong Way* (Ahmedabad, Navajivan, 1959).
[36] S. Radhakrishnan 'Inaugural address' *Proceedings of the Third International Conference on Planned Parenthood* (Bombay, 1952).

on the problem of the differential fertility of the various religious communities in India. And while some data on their attitudes towards and practice of contraception in India and elsewhere are available, information on abortion and its incidence among Muslim women is scarce. However, there is no reason to believe that the problems of fertility, morbidity and mortality among the Muslims and other minority communities in India are basically different from those of the Hindus.

What is the Islamic view of family planning and abortion? While the Hindu religion's attitude on any fundamental problem has to be drawn from a variety of scriptural texts and traditions, extant over many centuries, the Islamic attitude is easy to discover. Though there is no centralized Muslim spiritual hierarchy comparable to the Pope among the Catholics, the Muslims are required to find the answer to their problems firstly from the Holy Koran, secondly from the Hadith, (traditions from the Prophet Mohammed), and thirdly from the interpretations and opinions of Islamic ecclesiastical heads such as the *Muftis* and the *Ulamas*.

To begin with, the Muslims' attitude toward abortion should be examined against the background of their religious approach to population problems and family planning in general. And this approach must be viewed in the light of certain fundamental and well-known features of Islamic cultural, economic and social life as they have come down to the present day. These, as found in India and most Muslim countries, are the general social equality of all peoples, permissive polygamy (though restricted by certain states in their efforts at modernization), easy divorce, and the general backward status of women in religion but a relatively better status in personal law. Some of these features as well as certain traditions have encouraged a higher birth rate and large families in Islamic countries.[37]

As for family planning, some Islamic sayings give a clue to the general attitude: 'When a servant of Allah marries he perfects half his religion'; 'Marry and multiply so that I may be glorified in my community over other communities'. We remember how the disciples of Jesus disputed as to who should be the greatest. The Islamic version says that when the Companions disputed among themselves as to who was the best man, the Prophet replied, 'The best man is he who is a good husband'. Ibn Abbas said, 'Then marry, for the best man in our community is he who has most wives'.[38]

[37] The traditional Islamic view has been in opposition to birth control in general. The opposition is derived from the Koranic injunction, 'Murder not your children for fear lest ye be reduced to poverty. We will provide for you and them.' (Koran VI:151; XVII:31.)

[38] Arthur Jaffery, 'The Family in Islam', in Ruth Nanda Anshen (ed.), *The Family: Its Function and Destiny* (New York, Harper, 1949), p. 162.

It is known that coitus interruptus (*Azl* or *al-azh*) was practised widely by the Arabs for preventing unwanted pregnancies. It is believed that the Prophet allowed this practice. Abu Sayeed, a contemporary chronicler, relates: 'A man approached the Prophet and said, "Oh Messenger of Allah! I own a slave girl and practise *Azl* with her for I do not want her to be with child. I desire what men desire but the Jews say that *Azl* is minor infanticide." The Prophet replied, "The Jews are wrong. Indeed you can practise *Azl*. If Allah wills to create a child no one can prevent."'[39]

However, the fact that the Muslim faith has given in recent years a definitive and permissive ruling on contraception is not generally known. Islam, like Hinduism, and unlike Christianity, has no clergy, no church organization and no liturgy in the true sense of the term. Much of the personal law affecting birth, marriage, divorce and dowry is regulated according to the *Shariat* (Islamic law) and the *Fiqh* (Islamic jurisprudence). But when doubts arise, a Muslim can ask for a ruling on any specific question. More than thirty years ago such a doubt was submitted to His Worship the Grand Mufti of the Egyptian realm. The question was: What is Your Worship's opinion regarding the following?

A married man to whom one child was born is afraid that if several other children are born he would experience great hardship in rearing and providing for them, and that his health might suffer a nervous breakdown as a result of his exertions and worries. Or he may be afraid lest his wife's health might deteriorate as a result of repeated and frequent childbirths, without sufficient interval for birth and recuperation. Now, should he or his wife, under such circumstances, be allowed to take certain measures, recommended by medical men, to avoid frequent childbearing so that a long interval may pass between one childbirth and the next, in order that the mother may be rested and the father spared of any more hardship?

After a careful and detailed examination, particularly in the light of the Hanafy School of Law, the Grand Mufti issued a *fatwa* dated the 12th *Dhi al Quada* 1355 (25 January 1937). It runs: 'It is permissible for either husband or wife by mutual consent to take any measures ... in order to prevent conception.' (He refers to both natural and artificial methods.) He continues: 'Later scholars of the Hanafy School consider that such consent is not even necessary if either husband or wife has an excuse such as those mentioned or any similar ones.'

The problem of abortion was also considered and the *fatwa* adds:

Opinion on this subject has differed but the majority are inclined not to

[39] *Muslim Views on Family Planning* (Mysore, State Family Planning Bureau, 1969), p. 8.

allow it, except for a reason such as the interruption of the mother's milk when she has another baby and the father cannot afford a 'wet nurse' and the baby's life is therefore endangered. After the quickening of the embryo abortion is absolutely prohibited.[40]

Since the issue of this *fatwah* the Islamic theological view has undergone some change in keeping with modern needs and changing times. In December 1964, the Grand Mufti of Jordan stated, 'It is permissible to take medicine to procure abortion so long as the embryo is unformed in human shape'. This is interpreted as including induced abortion for therapeutic and other reasons, and the period of this unformed human state was given as 120 days.[41] 'It is evident,' says Dr Isam R. Nazer, 'that the Muslim religion is more permissive than either civil legislation or the Christian belief, as expressed by the British Council of Churches in its statement on human reproduction in 1962, suggesting that biological life becomes human life at the time of nidation.[42]

The official attitude of Pakistan, a Muslim country which has been tackling her population problems for some years now, has been to interpret the Islamic injunctions in the light of the nation's current economic and social needs. According to the Government of Pakistan:

Is family planning religiously acceptable? Islam, the most recent great religion of the world, not only takes care of the spiritual side of man, but also guides us regarding our relation with the universe, with life and with our fellow human beings. There is nothing in Islam which is alien to human nature. Thus man is completely free and responsible for his actions and self in the domain of his optional activities.

At no point does the Holy Koran raise any objection to the family planning practice. So far as the *sunnah* (or tradition) is concerned, birth control certainly appears to have been allowed by the Holy Prophet. There are specific statements in the Hadith that birth control used to be practised during the Holy Prophet's lifetime. The Holy Prophet knew of this but neither the Koran nor the Holy Prophet raised any specific objection to it. There are some reports to the contrary also but reliable and competent authorities have not considered these worthy of credence.

There are positive statements also from such leading Ulamas of Islam as Al-Ghazali and Ibn-Taimiyya, in favour of birth control. Indeed these

[40] In Arabic in the *Journal of the Egyptian Medical Association* (Cairo, July 1937). See also S. Chandrasekhar, *Population and Planned Parenthood in India*, 2nd edn. (London, Allen & Unwin, 1961), pp. 73-5; *News of Pupolation and Birth Control* (New York, May 1952).
[41] Isam R. Nazer, 'Abortion in the Near East', in Robert E. Hall (ed.), *Abortion in a Changing World*, vol. 1, p. 268.
[42] ibid. Today therapeutic abortion is permitted in Turkey, Iran, Egypt, Morocco and Tunisia. In other Muslim countries the ban exists in law but is seldom enforced and abortions are done in hospitals and clinics.

Ulamas have mentioned more than one form of birth control and have permitted it for the faithful.[43]

THE SOVIET UNION AND THE SOCIALIST COUNTRIES

While the Catholic Church took a totally uncompromising stand on contraception and abortion, the new communist society, on the other hand, took the other extreme view of permitting abortion for a variety of reasons, if not on mere demand. And yet for more than half a century the Catholic and communist ideologies have taken an identical view that population problems, as commonly understood, were basically a myth.

The first country in the world to legalize abortion was the Soviet Union. This was not done to meet any population problem (in the sense of an adverse ratio between total population and the available land and other natural resources at a given level of technology), for Marxist communism does not normally recognize the existence of a population problem in the Malthusian sense.

In the flush and new enthusiasm of the great 1917 revolution, the Russian leaders were for complete feminine equality and freedom. It was Lenin's strong belief that no woman in the new communist society should be forced to bear a child against her will, and that women should be assured the right of 'deciding for themselves a fundamental issue of their lives'. Thus the right of a Soviet woman to terminate an unwanted pregnancy on health and other grounds was recognized three years after the October 1917 revolution, in November 1920. Abortion became unrestricted and could be had virtually on demand in any abortion clinic or abortarium. In 1936, however, after a long public discussion, abortion was restricted to cases where there were medical and eugenic grounds for it, but this law was repealed in 1955 when abortion was again made available virtually on request.

The Soviet Union has reversed its decision on the legalization of abortion at least three times in the last half-century. The reasons for permitting abortion have been threefold. First, as pointed out already, Lenin and other leaders felt that the Soviet woman's freedom was of paramount importance in the new society. Secondly, as women were encouraged to enter factories and professions in large numbers and on equal terms with men, the state had to provide facilities for postponing motherhood, for preventing unwanted pregnancies and limiting the size of the family.

Last and perhaps the most important reason was the health of the

---

[43] *Family Planning Scheme for Pakistan during the Third Five Year Plan Period, 1965-70* (Karachi, Ministry of Health, Labour and Social Welfare, 1965), p. 148.

Russian woman. The pressing practical consideration was to prevent illegal abortions. Russian women, for a variety of reasons, including at the beginning a non-affluent, if not a harsh, environment, were resorting to criminal abortion with all its attendant evils of mutilation and even death at the hands of quacks. There is no doubt that the legalization of abortion has brought about a decline in criminal abortion in all the socialist countries. There has also been a corresponding decline in mortality and morbidity as a consequence of abortion.

While the permissive 1955 law on abortion is still in force today the Soviet Union has consistently encouraged women to resort to contraception instead of abortion. And this liberal attitude toward abortion has now become the law in all the socialist countries, all the way from Poland to China,[44] with only slight variations to meet particular national needs at various periods in the last few decades.[45]

After the Soviet Union, the Scandinavian countries began to liberalize their abortion laws in the 1930s. The reform began in Iceland in 1935 and was followed by Sweden in 1938 and Denmark in 1939. Finland and Norway either passed or codified similar laws in 1950 and 1960.

GREAT BRITAIN AND THE COMMONWEALTH

In Anglo-Saxon law induced abortion was an ecclesiastical offence, not a criminal one, until the reign of George III. The earliest English abortion statute, the law of 1803, made induced abortion a crime, but it was punishable by death only if it took place 'after quickening'. The penalty for earlier abortions was imprisonment or transportation for up to fourteen years.

The statutes enacted in the late eighteenth and early nineteenth

[44] Communist China legalized abortion and made it available virtually on request from May 1957. Statistics on the number of legal abortions performed are, however, not available. During a visit to Peking in 1959 I was informed by the Communist health authorities that a well-known Chinese actress was included in a Chinese cultural delegation going to Africa. When she informed the concerned authorities that she was three months pregnant she was advised to obtain an abortion and join the delegation.
See Edgar Snow, *The Long Revolution* (New York, Random House, 1972), pp. 31–34.
[45] The Marxist philosophy of the freedom of women as interpreted by Lenin is so widespread that abortion is available for the usual indications in the Mongolian People's Republic. The writer, during a brief sojourn there in 1969, was informed by the health authorities in Ulan Bator that while there was no population problem in either the demographic or the Marxist sense, the Mongolian woman could obtain an abortion as easily as the Russian woman, despite the fact that the nation, half the size of India, supports fewer than two million people, and could possibly support more at the present level of living.

centuries continued to distinguish between an abortion procured before quickening and one performed after. (According to Aristotelian law, the mother felt quickening of life in the womb after forty days in the case of a male and eighty days in the case of a female infant. And Aristotle, of course, did not tell us how foetal sex was to be determined.) It was not till 1861 that England passed legislation against abortion without reference to the time of gestation.

The English common law on abortion took shape in the middle of the nineteenth century during Queen Victoria's reign, when in 1861 Britain passed the Offences Against the Person Act, section 58 of which made abortion at any time a crime punishable by a maximum penalty of life imprisonment. English law, however, defined induced abortion as interruption of pregnancy after quickening had occurred. It is on this law that most of the statutes prohibiting abortion in the former British Empire and the United States of America were based. The first breach in this law was made by the Infant Life Preservation Act of 1929, which permitted a doctor to terminate a pregnancy to save a woman's life.

However, it is generally not known that Great Britain pioneered in attempting to reform the law on abortion, as she has pioneered in introducing most progressive laws in the world among the English-speaking countries. In 1937, seventeen years after the Soviet Union liberalized her abortion law, Great Britain appointed an Interdepartmental Committee (Ministry of Health and the Home Office) under the chairmanship of Sir Norman (later Lord) Birkett, KC, to inquire into the whole subject of illegal abortions in Great Britain and suggest reforms. The report of this committee was published in 1939. It estimated that the total number of illegal abortions performed in England and Wales every year ranged from 45,000 to 60,000, and noted that between 400 and 600 women died from these illegal operations, or 'causes attributed to or associated with illegal abortion'.

The report conceded that 'the law in this matter is freely disregarded among women of all types and classes, in many cases with subsequent misery and ill health . . . [we] regard this state of affairs as a great social evil'. But having conceded that the evil existed and that something ought to be done about it, the report unfortunately became obsessed with the fear of Britain's falling birth rate and beat a retreat from any bold advocacy of abortion reform. The Committee not only did not recommend liberalization of Britain's abortion law but, on the contrary, expressed itself against making contraception widely available. The report trotted out the then current, if irrational, fear of a decline in population: 'A proposal that public money should be spent on a measure which is likely to aggravate this position [declining birth rate] by making contraception universally available on request, and thereby to affect adversely the continuity of the State, is one which we feel we cannot endorse.'

Then came the problem of sexual morals. 'An additional objection to an official campaign of this nature [the spread of contraceptive facilities] is that it would tend to lower the traditional and accepted standards of sexual morality in this country.... We believe that contraceptive knowledge may often be a source of temptation.' In fairness to the Committee, however, it must be added that it referred to the Bourne trial, which had been engaging the attention of the British public at that time. The trial's result was a landmark in the sense that it liberalized the case law on abortion.

The story of the famous case *Bourne* v. *the Crown* may be briefly told. A 14-year-old English girl had been watching the changing of the guard at the Palace of Whitehall in London. After the event she accepted the invitation of two troopers to see a remarkable curiosity, 'a horse with a green tail'. When she entered the stables she was dragged to a barracks room where she was held by five associates and assaulted by two soldiers. The two soldiers were later identified and imprisoned.

When it was discovered that the girl was pregnant the case was referred to Dr Alec Bourne, a distinguished British gynaecologist. With parental consent she was admitted to St Mary's Hospital, where after a week's observation to study the impact of the assault on her physical and mental health, Dr Bourne performed an abortion. That evening two police officers called on him at the hospital and warned him against performing the abortion. The doctor replied that he had already performed the operation, 'as in my opinion as an obstetrical surgeon, it may be dangerous to a girl of her age to bear a full term child'.

At the trial, Dr Bourne testified: 'I cannot draw a line between danger to life and danger to health. If we waited for danger to life, the woman is past assistance....' The doctor believed that apart from the trauma of the assault it was dangerous for a girl of her age to bear a child. '[Her pregnancy] would sooner or later undermine her physical health and produce physical symptoms.... When I am speaking of derangement of the nervous system, I know and most medical men know that it sooner or later would undermine her physical health and produce symptoms which may wreck her whole life. Ninety-nine per cent of my colleagues would be agreeable to an operation such as I performed.'

As Lawrence Lader points out, 'Justice Macnaughten's summary to the jury made two points, clearly a landmark in medico-legal history: "Life depends on health"; and "It may be that if health is gravely impaired, death results."' Furthermore, he declared, only the physician has the responsibility of deciding this danger. 'The law is not that the doctor has got to wait until this unfortunate woman is in peril of immediate death and then at the last moment, if successful, snatch her from the jaws of death.'[46] Dr Bourne was, of course, acquitted.

It was thus that the interpretation based on the Bourne case became case law. After that seven attempts, all unsuccessful, were made to introduce reformed abortion legislation in the British Parliament.[47] In October 1967 the old law on abortion was liberalized with the enactment of the new Abortion Act[48] which came into force on 27 April 1968.

THE NEW CLIMATE IN THE UNITED STATES

Despite the pioneering role of the Soviet Union (and other socialist countries in Europe and Asia) in liberalizing abortion laws half a century ago, and Japan's permissive Eugenics Protection Law of 1948, the Christian world of Europe and America continued to ban abortion. Even a serious popular discussion of the subject was more or less taboo. For instance, in the United States of America, where different states have different laws, a man could be convicted of rape and sent to prison but his victim could not obtain a legal abortion to end her unwanted pregnancy.

But something strange happened in the mid-sixties. A wave of loud dissent from the women's liberation movement, and protests from legal, medical and demographic experts swept the United States. The time for change had arrived. During the year 1967 alone four states, Colorado, North Carolina, California and even Mississippi, altered their restrictive abortion statutes. By the end of 1972 sixteen states had liberalized, and more than half of the remaining states were reviewing their antiquated abortion laws. It is probable that within a decade or so enlightened public opinion in the United States will not tolerate the hypocrisy of politicians who permit tons of bombs to be dropped on enemy targets killing countless people, but pretend to get perturbed over the 'rights of the unborn'.[49]

[46] For details of Britain's struggle for abortion reform see Lawrence Lader, *Abortion*, 2nd edn. (Boston, Beacon Press, 1967), pp. 103-10.

[47] The Bill which became the Abortion Act 1967 was sponsored by David Steel, Liberal MP. Seven earlier unsuccessful Bills on the subject had been presented by Joseph Reeves in 1952, Lord Amulree, 1954, Kenneth Robinson, 1961, Renee Short, 1965, Lord Silkin, 1965 and 1966 and Simon Wingfield Digby, 1965.

[48] For various British medical comments on the Act see *The Abortion Act 1967*, proceedings of a symposium held by the Medical Protection Society (London, Pitman, 1969).

[49] The US Presidential Commission on Population Growth (Rockefeller Com-

THE INCIDENCE OF ABORTION

A survey of the world abortion situation from the available evidence reveals that abortion has been the most widely practised method of fertility control in virtually every country, no matter what its culture, politics or religion.

While it is difficult to come by reliable data, a rough estimate suggests that every year more than 35 million women have induced abortions, legal and illegal, and a great majority of these in furtive and unhygienic surroundings by back street abortionists. That is, every day nearly 100,000 women prefer facing possible mutilation, disaster and even death to bringing their pregnancies to term, obviously for a variety of very good reasons.

It is difficult to break up this global educated estimate in terms of national statistics, because except for a few countries where abortion is legal, national official statistical yearbooks do not include this item. Certain *ad hoc* surveys and sample studies, however, give a clue to the magnitude of abortion in certain countries.

In the Soviet Union, according to Dr K. H. Mehlan,[50] some 6 million abortions take place every year. While no official figure has

---

mission Report) has published a report which points out the sexual permissiveness among the young in the USA. Surveying young women between the ages of 15 and 19 it reaches the conclusion that nearly half of all unmarried American girls have had sexual experience, although most of these have had only one partner, and the experience has not been frequent. More than three-quarters of the young women have never used contraceptives or have used them only sometimes, thus running high risks of becoming pregnant. The statistics reveal that at the age of 19, some 80·8 per cent of black women, 40·4 per cent of white women and 27·6 per cent of other ethnic groups have had sexual experience, reinforcing, says the report, 'our idea about the appalling risk of pregnancy run by many teenage girls'. The report also observes that 'While proportionately more blacks than whites have had intercourse, it is the white non-virgins who ... are the more promiscuous'. See *Population and the American Future: The Report of the Commission on Population Growth and the American Future* (New York, New American Library, 1972), *passim*.

The Commission recommended that contraceptive services and information be provided to teenagers. However, the suggestion has met with cold disapproval from President Nixon. 'Such measures', he said, 'would do nothing to preserve and strengthen close family relations.' Some experts on American sexual delinquent behaviour have asked the President what the present arrangements – that is to say, pregnancy among schoolgirls and secret abortions performed by quacks in garages – are doing to strengthen close family ties.

[50] K. H. Mehlan, 'Changing Patterns of Abortion in the Socialist Countries of Europe', in Robert E. Hall (ed.), *Abortion in a Changing World* (New York, Columbia University Press, 1970).

been published in the People's Republic of China, the total number of abortions is believed to be about 5 million per year. In Hungary,[51] the official estimates put the total number of abortions as exceeding 100,000 a year. While Hungary has an extremely liberal abortion law, some women still resort to illegal abortion.

Since the peak year of 1955 when 2 million abortions were performed, the incidence of abortion in Japan has been declining gradually, possibly for the twin reasons of more widespread use of contraception and the government's pronounced fear of a labour shortage. In India, before the liberal law of 1971 was passed, there were according to an official estimate some 5 million abortions a year. In the United States of America, before the present liberal abortion laws in some states were passed, estimates of induced abortion ranged from 700,000 to 2,000,000 a year. And according to Thomlinson's summary of several studies in the 1960s 'about one out of every five pregnancies of the United States terminates in illegal abortion'.[52] The estimate of illegal abortions in West Germany for 1967 ranges between 1 and 3 millions. In great Britain, before the 1967 Act was passed, an estimate put the total number of induced abortions at 100,000 a year. In Canada, the annual figure is about 50,000.

As for Catholic countries, a few random examples should suffice. Italy probably leads the list with an estimated 650,000 to 900,000 illegal abortions in 1967, while for France the average annual figure varies between 250,000 and 300,000. Of the 200,000 abortions that take place in Chile annually, two-thirds are induced. According to a hospital survey, one out of every four Chilean women has had at least one illegal abortion; in Mexico it is one out of every three women. Illegal abortions in Argentina and Uruguay in 1967 totalled 500,000 and 100,000 respectively. For Belgium the estimate is more than 100,000 a year.[53]

These figures convey the magnitude of the problem. So long as these induced abortions are illegal the utter misery and possible morbidity can only be imagined.

---

[51] Egon Szabady, 'Family Planning Trends: The Hungarian Study', *Demografia* II (1968). See also Henry P. David, *Family Planning and Abortion in the Socialist Countries of Central and Eastern Europe* (New York, The Population Council, 1970), *passim*.

[52] William Petersen, *Population*, 2nd edn. (New York, Macmillan, 1969), p. 187; also R. Thomlinson, *Population Dynamics* (New York, Random House, 1965), p. 198.

[53] For data on hospital admissions for abortions, legal and illegal abortions, and ratio of abortions per 1,000 births for selected countries for latest available years see *International Consultants' Report 1970*, a special project of the Association for the Study of Abortion (New York, 1970).

METHODS OF ABORTION

Many have been the primitive, painful and dangerous methods used for abortion. Millions of women through the centuries have followed old wives' tales about drugs that produce abortion. No drug, however, has yet been made that can be taken by mouth to produce an abortion. The folklore of some ancient cultures has recommended various Charms and talismans, leaves and barks, roots and fruits to abort an early foetus.[54] No medical research body has tested all these beliefs based on herbal remedies. Such drugs as ergot and quinine have proved just as unsuccessful as herbs. Violent physical exercise, such as galloping on horseback or jumping from a chair, has also proved of no avail. Lastly there are the women who tamper with their uteruses with a variety of things, infect themselves and bleed to death.

In the early stages of pregnancy, within the first trimester, the standard method of operation adopted is the D and C (dilation and curettage). The patient's womb is reached through the vagina and opened with a series of graduated little cone-shaped surgical instruments called dilators. The first dilator is no bigger in diameter than a soda straw, the next is a little larger and so on until the opening of the womb is wide enough to permit the insertion of a small surgical instrument called a curette or an ovum forceps. The curette is used to scrape the wall of the womb gently to dislodge the embryo and the placenta. What has been loosened is removed from the uterus with the aid of a tweezer-like instrument, the ovum forceps. While curettage is not painful, as there are no nerve endings in the uterus, dilatation of the cervix is painful, hence the need for anaesthesia.

When this simple surgical procedure is done under anaesthesia by a competent surgeon in a well-equipped hospital, nothing should go amiss. The operation is normally completed in about fifteen minutes with a minimum loss of blood. The patient is up after a few hours and hospitalization is needed for only two or three days.

[54] The common Indian rural technique for abortion is to employ the services of a local midwife. For a fee of about ten rupees she will insert a carefully selected twig of the *erukku* (Tamil) plant (*Calotropis gigantea*) into the pregnant woman's cervix. It is believed that if the woman is about six weeks pregnant she will abort within a day or two and recover quite quickly. If she is closer to three months pregnant it is supposed to take two to three days for the uterus to expel the foetus, and she may take a fortnight to recover. Though the juice of this plant is highly poisonous, the present writer has not heard of any fatal case when the technique is properly administered. Some medical researcher might look into this and decide whether the contention is valid.

In Latin America the insertion of a parsley stem into the cervix appears to be the most popular method of induced abortion.

A new medical technique, abortion by suction or aspiration, has been perfected in the Soviet Union. Today this method has come into vogue in many parts of the world besides the communist countries. The suction pump[55] is really a simple device based on the vacuum principle. A sterile hollow metal tube (with a little window-like aperture on the side near its tip) is inserted through the cervix to reach the top of the uterine cavity. This hollow aspirator is then connected by transparent plastic tubing to a suction bottle. The suction pump (which can be worked either mechanically or manually) is then started, reaching between 1/2 and 1 atm of negative pressure. While gently sweeping the aspirator around the uterus the surgeon can tell when he has made contact with the embryo by observing the bits of foetal matter that appear in the transparent tubing. The aspirator is worked over the area in the uterus where the embryo is attached until all the tissue has been sucked into the tubing. The operation lasts no more than three or four minutes with only a slight loss of blood.[56]

[55] M. Vojta, 'A Critical View of Vacuum Aspiration: A New Method for the Termination of Pregnancy', *Obstetrics and Gynaecology*, (July 1967).
[56] In 1969 the writer, during one of his visits to the Soviet Union to study her abortion laws, was invited by Dr Boris Petrovsky, the distinguished surgeon and Soviet Minister for Public Health, to watch an abortion by vacuum aspiration. After a twenty-mile drive by car from Moscow we reached a nursing home located in the centre of attractive wooded countryside. In the large, cheerfully furnished drawing room we were received by two surgeons, one of whom was the Director of the abortion clinic. Some thirty women – ages ranging roughly between twenty and forty-five – were in the drawing room sipping tea, watching television and chatting. They were patients waiting their turn for abortion. While normally the Soviet system does not permit any intrusion into the Soviet woman's freedom or privacy, I was kindly permitted to ask the women any questions I might have. I asked the youngest-looking patient why she needed an abortion. She replied that she was a married student at the Moscow State University and lived in cramped married students' quarters. The contraceptive had failed and she was anxious to finish her studies before she became a mother. Apart from the inconvenience to her husband, also a student, the apartment did not have space for a baby. 'After graduation, both of us will get jobs and move into a larger apartment when I shall have a baby', she concluded in a matter of fact fashion. As I went around, I found that every woman had some personal problem necessitating an abortion. The last one I talked to was a healthy woman in her forties. She said, 'I am a factory worker and have married children. My contraceptive failed and I am too old and rather too tired to think of rearing a new baby now'.

The surgeon asked whose turn it was and while she went off with a junior physician to be prepared for the operation, the surgeon and I, after donning white coats, went upstairs to the operating room where a patient under anaesthesia was wheeled in. The surgeon suggested I time the operation and watch the minimal loss of blood.

When the operation was over I noticed that it had taken exactly three minutes. After lunch, the Soviet surgeon and I visited the patient. She was out of anaesthesia, was feeling relieved and happy, and wondered whether she could go home to her children that evening. The surgeon asked her to stay in the nursing home for a day

The D and C and the vacuum aspirator are normally used to abort a pregnancy less than three months old. If a later pregnancy has to be aborted these two methods are of no use. The foetus is too large to be evacuated through a dilated cervix or removed by suction. The abortion of a later pregnancy is done by an abdominal operation called a hysterotomy or miniature Caesarean section. With a longitudinal incision on the lower abdomen, the uterus is opened and the foetus is removed just as a baby is delivered by Caesarean section.

During the last decade Sweden has perfected a new method for aborting pregnancies between fourteen and twenty-two weeks. Some seven ounces of the amniotic fluid that surrounds the foetus are withdrawn by means of a needle thrust through the abdominal wall into the uterine cavity, and are replaced with an equal quantity of a 20 per cent salt (sodium chloride) or 50 per cent glucose solution. Labour normally commences after twenty-four hours and the patient is able to expel both the foetus and the placenta, which has been killed by the hypertonic solution. This relatively simple method has begun to replace the abdominal surgery of hysterotomy.

We have come a long way from the abortifacient prescriptions of potions and poisons of the pre-Christian era to the Soviet suction pump. From primitive miserable methods which mean mutilation, prolonged morbidity and even death, the present abortion methods are so safe and simple that it is no more hazardous than a tooth extraction. In fact, today a hospital abortion is safer than childbirth itself.

What of the future? There is no doubt that there will be near-miraculous scientific answers to some of these problems in the near future. There is really no need for new knowledge but only for an assiduous application of the already available knowledge in a dozen disciplines. It is simply a question of priorities and bringing men, materials and money together to find an ideal contraceptive—cheap, simple, safe, sure and culturally acceptable. And then abortion could become a thing of the past, for there would be no unwanted pregnancies. Should such a contraceptive ever fail and the resulting unwanted pregnancy need to be terminated, the science of the future should be able to provide a device even better and simpler than the suction pump. Dr Carl Djerassi summarizes the possibilities thus:

A shot to immunize women against pregnancy, a pill to render men temporarily sterile and a monthly pill to ensure a regular monthly flow may all be in common use within the next decade.

---

or two and then go home when she was completely recovered. I have observed even in remote rural areas the extremely competent and adequate medical care that the Soviet Union gives its citizens, particularly the women and children.

The contraceptive pill for man may be only four or five years away, depending upon the level of funding and political attractiveness.

The prostaglandins, more than anything else now in sight, herald an entirely new generation of contraceptives, a generation that is destined to make the pill seem as dated as the diaphragm, as clumsy and unappealing as the condom. Every woman can now look forward to simpler, safer, surer contraception in the years ahead.

Given the current interest in the study of reproductive physiology and methods of contraception, I think it is very likely that in a relatively short time – five to fifteen years – scientists will discover ways of controlling the fertility of an entire population.[57]

Thus the future is full of hope, once the political climate, a certain religious obscurantism and the cultural milieu of the developed countries permit the emergence of such innovation. A society that can put a man on the moon – in terms of both funding and technology - can give itself and the world an ideal contraceptive and abortion technique and avert the current and possibly worsening future global demographic disaster.

ABORTION IN INDIA

In a country such as India where vital registration – a bare record of births, marriages and deaths – is far from being accurate, complete or reliable and where the magnitude of the under-registration of births varies between 5 and 10 per cent in certain States of the Union, it would be unreasonable to expect any official figures on abortion. Figures are not even available on spontaneous abortions (which are often brought to the attention of the medical profession), much less on induced abortions, which except for therapeutic reasons have been illegal in the recent past. For obvious reasons it is difficult to offer even a realistic estimate. This difficulty is true of most parts of the world. However, some 'guesstimates' based on certain assumptions are available. On the basis of these it is believed that some 30 million abortions take place in the world every year.[58] Other estimates range up to 40 million.[59]

As for India, some information has been collected from a variety of scattered sources, such as maternity hospital statistics, histories of obstetrical patients, records of family planning clinics, and *ad hoc*

---

[57] The quotes are assembled by Professor Carl Djerassi, 'Fertility Control through Abortion: An Assessment of the Period 1950–1980', *Bulletin of the Atomic Scientists* (January 1972).

[58] E. Haneman and the editors of *Life*, *Birth Control* (New York, Time-International, 1967), pp. 93–103.

[59] Professor Carl Djerassi believes that the total number of abortions in the world is in the neighbourhood of about 40 million (see *Bulletin of the Atomic Scientists*).

community health surveys. A review of the available Indian secondary data and survey reports gives a rough idea of the magnitude and variation of abortion rates in rural and urban population. Of the eleven urban and four rural studies available, four of the urban studies were based on an analysis of clinical records on abortions, while the data for the remaining studies were derived from community surveys.

These studies and consequently their findings are not really comparable for several reasons. They were poorly designed and no acceptable sampling techniques were employed. Both the methods employed and the demographic and socio-economic characteristics of the 'samples' varied. The abortion rates obtained from urban clinical records are higher than the rates obtained from rural surveys and these are not comparable for understandable reasons: the urban women readily seek medical services with the result that the records in the clinics are relatively better kept; and urban women with complications during pregnancy more frequently seek medical care than women who do not experience such complications. On the other hand, pregnant women in rural areas do not have comparable facilities; nor are they educated to seek and utilize such facilities as are available. Further, virtually all abortions in rural areas, spontaneous and induced, are not attended by even paramedical personnel. And lastly, all these findings are not comparable, for in some cases the base for computing the percentage of abortions is a hundred pregnancies while for others it is a hundred live births.

Rural Studies

A demographic and family planning study of a rural population of about 12,000 in Khanna District in the Punjab State over a period of about five years was carried out in the nineteen-sixties. The data obtained through prospective field observations of 1,765 pregnancies gave an overall rate of 100 abortions per 1,000 pregnancies. This was considered an underestimate in view of several known limiting factors.[60]

In 1951, as part of a general population survey of Bangalore City and certain small villages of Mysore State covering a sample of 1,403 married women and 1,084 husbands, a Fertility and Attitude Survey was carried out under the joint auspices of the United Nations and the Ministry of Health of the Government of India. The report, which was published in 1961, obtained an abortion rate of 41 per 1,000 pregnancies in the rural population as against a rate of 79

[60] R. G. Potter *et al*, 'Foetal Wastage in Eleven Punjab Villages', *Human Biology*, (September 1965).

abortions per 1,000 pregnancies in Bangalore City.[61] These figures are believed to be underestimates, although the extent of underestimation could not be determined.

The following table shows abortion rates by age of mother in eleven Punjab villages, 1955–9.

Table 1. Foetal Deaths by Mothers' Age, 1955–1959

Age of mother (at last menstrual period)	Total pregnancies	Total deaths per 1,000 pregnancies	Rate under 4 months (early abortions)	Rate 4–6 months (late abortions)	Rate 7 or more months (still births)
15–19	141	191·4	70·9	61·1	73·2
20–24	480	120·8	64·6	57·9	23·1
25–29	495	105·0	42·4	23·2	43·2
30–34	335	125·4	71·0	41·8	16·8
35–39	210	171·4	104·8	21·5	54·3
40 and over	104	240·4	182·7	47·0	24·7
Total	1765	156·0	72·0	34·8	35·4

Another study of six rural communities in Maharashtra State undertaken by the Gokhale Institute of Politics and Economics, Poona, between 1951 and 1956, revealed an abortion rate of 25 per 1,000 pregnancies. The study, which covered a population of about 38,000, offers no explanation for what is apparently a low rate in comparison with figures obtained for areas elsewhere in the country.[62]

Yet another rural study, from Gandhigram, Madurai District, Madras State (Tamil Nadu), is based on maternity statistics in the project area and the Kasturba Maternity Hospital at Gandhigram, covering a population of roughly 20,000. The data collected for 1959 revealed that 12·7 per cent of all pregnancies recorded ended in spontaneous or induced abortions; that is, about 127 out of 1000 pregnancies were interrupted for various reasons.[63]

Gandhigram's Institute of Rural Health and Family Planning conducted an inquiry, similar to the above study but restricted to the

[61] *The Mysore Population Study* (New York, United Nations, 1961), p. 236.
[62] Kumidini Dandekar, *Demographic Survey of Six Rural Communities* (Poona, Gokhale Institute of Politics and Economics, 1959), p. 2.
[63] 'A Report on the Incidence of Abortion as studied from the data compiled at the Kasturba Maternity Hospital, Gandhigram', in *Quarterly Bulletin of the Pilot Health Project* (Gandhigram, October 1961).

Table 2. Incidence of Natural and Induced Abortions, Average Parity and Month of Pregnancy at which Aborted, by Women of Different Age Groups. Data for the Period 1-1-60 to 28-2-63.

Age group	No. in sample	No. of live births for these women from 1-1-60	Natural abortions					Induced abortions			
			No. of abortions reported from 1-1-60	Incidence rate[1]	Average parity of abortion[2]	Average month of pregnancy at the time of abortion	No. of abortions reported from 1-1-60	Incidence rate[1]	Average parity of abortion[2]	Average month of pregnancy at the time of abortion
20–22	9	9	2	22·2	3·0	3·5	1	11·1	3·0	3·0
23–25	15	18	1	5·6	4·0	4·0	5	27·8	4·0	2·4
26–28	26	37	5	13·5	5·6	3·0	2	5·4	7·0	2·5
29–31	20	23	4	17·4	5·5	3·5	11	47·8	6·5	2·5
32–34	6	4	3	75·0	8·0	3·7	4	100·0	8·5	3·0
35–37	13	9	7	77·8	8·3	2·4	2	22·2	9·0	2·0
38–40	11	5	1	20·0	11·0	2·0	7	140·0	10·4	3·1
Total	100	105	23	21·9	6·7	2·8	32	30·5	7·3	2·7

[1] Expressed in relation to 100 live births.
[2] Parity defined as order of pregnancy (including live births, still births and abortions).

small community of weavers in the same area, into the incidence of abortion for a three-year period between 1960 and 1963. This study, which was confined to a sample of 100 women below 40 who were mothers of 2 or more live births, revealed a natural abortion rate of 21·9 per 100 live births and an induced abortion rate of 30·5 per 100 live births.[64]

While this study was restricted to a small community and a small sample it showed that the incidence of abortion – natural and induced – increased with a rise in the age of the mother. Secondly, it was also found that the mother who had an easy and successful experience with the first induced abortion was more likely to come for a second induced abortion than the woman seeking abortion for the first time.

Urban Studies

The results of a few surveys on abortion in urban areas in India are available and these are confined to the major cities of Bombay, Calcutta and Delhi. Much of the information on abortion in these cities has been obtained as a by-product of other studies.

The Family Planning Training and Research Centre in Bombay found from their records of family planning clinics in 1960, comprising 1,227 cases, a total of 3,858 conceptions. Of these 299 pregnancies (7·8 per cent) had ended in abortion, 216 (5·6 per cent) spontaneously and 83 (2·2 per cent) induced.[65]

Some information on the incidence of abortion for Bombay City was obtained in a fertility survey carried out by the Demographic Training and Research Centre in Greater Bombay in 1960. The study was based on interviews with a sample of 7,872 married women in the reproductive age group. Of the reported total of 26,008 lifetime pregnancies, 1,503 were terminated in abortions—presumably both spontaneous and induced. This reveals an abortion rate of 5·8 per 1,000 pregnancies. When the analysis of pregnancies, however, was restricted to one year, 1964–5, it was found that there were 1,309 pregnancies, of which 92 were terminated in abortions, yielding an abortion rate of 7·05 for 100 pregnancies.[66]

In Calcutta, an analysis of the records of 929 patients in the maternity department of the R. G. Kar Medical College and Hospital,

[64] 'A Report on the Incidence of Abortion in a Weaver Community in the Project Area', *Quarterly Bulletin of the Pilot Health Project* Gandhigram (July 1963).
[65] Sarah Israel, *Some Observations on Abortion* (Bombay, Family Planning Training and Research Centre, 1967); mimeographed paper.
[66] Asha Bende, *Abortion Rates among the Currently Married Women in Greater Bombay* (Bombay, Demographic Training and Research Centre, 1967); mimeographed paper.

Calcutta in 1957 revealed a total of 3,541 pregnancies. The data showed an abortion rate of 15·07 per 100 pregnancies.[67]

The Delhi Demographic Research Centre carried out a survey of abortion among the wives of the 2,830 railway workers at the Kishanganj Railway Colony in Delhi.[68] It was a low income group—the workers earned salaries between Rs 100 and 500 a month. Out of a total of 11,897 pregnancies, 1,267 were aborted, giving an abortion rate of 10·6 per 100 pregnancies. The spontaneous and induced abortion rates worked out at 9·3 and 1·3 per 100 pregnancies respectively. This study also yielded the following conclusions:

1. The tendency to abort was higher in young ages (below 20 years) and in relatively higher age groups (30 years and above). The abortion rate for the age group 20–30 years was about 8 while for higher age groups it ranged between 10 and 20 per 100 pregnancies.
2. The higher the order of pregnancy the higher the abortion rate. Among pregnancies after the 12th the abortion rate was as high as 28·7 per 100 pregnancies.
3. Induced abortion was more prevalent among the higher than the lower income groups.
4. The induced abortion rate had a direct relation to the standard of schooling and general education of both the husband and the wife. The higher the education, the higher was the rate of induced abortion.

In New Delhi an analysis of the abortion cases admitted to the Lady Hardinge Medical College Hospital over a period of eight years (1956–63) showed that of a total of 1,201 admissions, 682 were either full term or premature deliveries, and the rest terminated in abortion, revealing one abortion for every three deliveries. In the analysis of 1,908 cases admitted for abortion, 47·5 per cent were in the age group 25–34 years. The ratio of abortions to pregnancies among the 110 women interviewed was 39·5 for every 100 pregnancies.[69]

Another study in Delhi was based on an examination of the records of women attending family planning clinics. During 1955–58, 5,912 women visited eight Delhi family planning clinics. Their histories revealed an abortion rate of 10·2 per 100 pregnancies for the pre-clinic period, that is, before these women visited the clinics for family planning advice or services. The abortion rate after visits to the

[67] S. Mukherjee and S. Biswas, 'Previous abortions and their relationship to current terminations and socio-economic status based on hospital data', *The Journal of Obstetrics and Gynaecology of India* (September 1959).
[68] R. P. Goyal, *A Study of Abortions among Railway Workers in Delhi* (Delhi, Demographic Research Centre, Institute of Economic Growth, no date); mimeographed paper.
[69] D. Anand, 'Clinico-Epidemiological Study of Abortion', *The Licentiate* (Ambala, October 1965).

clinics almost doubled and was 20·3 per 100 pregnancies. Apparently, women who are highly motivated to practise contraception for limiting the size of their families resort to abortion when the contraceptives used prove unsuccessful.[70]

In brief, of the 30 to 40 million[71] abortions that are presumed to occur in the world every year, some 6·5 million are believed to take place in India (2·6 million spontaneous and 3·9 induced). The Report of the Abortion Committee points out:

Some guesses can be made on the magnitude of the problem. If it is assumed that for every 73 live births 25 abortions take place of which 15 are induced, the number of abortions annually in a 1,000 population may be approximately 13·5 natural and 8 induced (corresponding to the estimated birth rate of 39). In a population of 500 million the number of abortions per year will be 6·5 million, 2·6 million natural and 3·9 million induced.[72]

If these figures and those cited earlier are accepted for whatever they are worth, it is probable that the total number of induced abortions in India in a year is in the neighbourhood of five million.

If the approximate figure of 5 million induced abortions is accepted the problem of how many of these pregnant women are incapacitated or killed in the process of an illegal abortion by back street 'doctors' and quacks and dirty-fingernailed *dais* (midwives) under insanitary and unhygienic conditions is a moot point. If this estimate is correct the nation loses thousands of women, most of them married and mothers, every year through crude and miserable attempts at abortion. The tragic loss of these women to the nation can hardly be overestimated. If the average woman has five children (since an overwhelming majority of women are married), countless children and adolescents are rendered motherless every year. An incredibly sad and shameful situation to say the least.

As for the mothers left incapacitated and mutilated there is no way of estimating the magnitude of their number or the depth of their plight. And as for cost, if an average expenditure of no more than Rs. 100 per induced abortion is assumed (a very conservative figure), the annual expenditure on induced abortions may be Rs. 500 million.

[70] A. N. Agarwala, 'Abortion Rate among a Section of Delhi's Population', *Medical Digest* (Bombay, January 1962).
[71] See Carl Djerassí, op. cit.
[72] *Report of the Committee to Study the Question of Legalization of Abortion* (New Delhi, Ministry of Health and Family Planning, 1966), p. 18.

THE PRE-1971 INDIAN LAW ON ABORTION

The Indian Penal Code (IPC) was enacted a little over a century ago in 1860 in conformity with the British law of that time. Prior to August 1971 induced abortion was illegal in India.

The old law on abortion is contained in sections 312 and 314 of the Indian Penal Code. Section 312 makes 'causing miscarriage' an offence. Sections 313 and 314 deal with aggravated forms of the offence. Section 312 reads as follows:

Whoever voluntarily causes a woman with child to miscarry shall, if such miscarriage be not caused in good faith for the purpose of saving the life of the woman, be punished with imprisonment of either description for a term which may extend to three years, or with fine, or with both; and if the woman be quick with child, shall be punished with imprisonment of either description for a term which may extend to seven years, and shall also be liable to fine.

Explanation: A woman who causes herself to miscarry is within the meaning of this section.

This section requires two essentials, (1) voluntarily causing a woman with child to miscarry, and (2) that such miscarriage should not have been caused in good faith for the purpose of saving the life of the woman. The offender may be the woman herself or any other person. The only case in which causing miscarriage is permitted is when it is done in good faith for the purpose of saving the life of the woman. If it is done under any other circumstances, the person causing the miscarriage will be guilty of the offence of causing miscarriage. An attempt to cause miscarriage is also punishable under the law. In a prosecution for causing miscarriage, the prosecution has to prove that the woman was with child; that the accused performed some act likely to cause miscarriage; that the accused did so voluntarily; that the woman did miscarry in consequence and that such miscarriage was not caused in good faith in order to save the woman's life.

In Great Britain, however, the law which was similar to the Indian law was amended in 1967. The 1967 amended British law includes the statement:

A person shall not be guilty of an offence under the law relating to abortion when a pregnancy is terminated by a registered medical practitioner if two registered medical practitioners are of the opinion formed in good faith:
(a) that the continuance of the pregnancy would involve risk to the life of the pregnant woman or any existing children of her family, greater than if the pregnancy were not terminated; or

(b) that there is a substantial risk that if the child were born it would suffer from such physical or mental abnormalities as to be seriously handicapped.

In determining whether the continuance of a pregnancy would involve such risk of injury to health as is mentioned in paragraph (a) of the subsection (1) of this section, account may be taken of the pregnant woman's actual or foreseeable environment.[73]

In India, however, section 312 of the Indian Penal Code remained unchanged till the new Act was passed in 1971.

[73] *Abortion Act, 1967* (London, HMSO, 1967), 87, p. 1.

Chapter 2

India's Population Problem

INTRODUCTION

Of all the problems confronting man in the last third of the twentieth century, perhaps none is more grave or disturbing in the long run than man's uncontrolled fertility. It is conceded by all thoughtful citizens and progressive governments that an excessive rate of population growth – in various regions, nations, and in the world as a whole – is the greatest single man-made barrier in the path of overall planned economic and social development and the achievement of a harmonious ecological balance between man and his total environment. And nowhere is the pressure of numbers on the available limited resources greater than in contemporary India, which continues to be the 'locus classicus' of the Malthusian dilemma.[1]

Today the total world population has passed three and a half thousand million and there seem to be no signs that this population growth will taper off in the near future. It increased at a faster rate during the first half of this century – and even faster during the last two decades – than ever before in human history. It took all the vast stretch of time from the emergence of Cro-Magnon man some 30,000 years ago to the beginning of the Christian era for the world's population to reach about 250 million. By about 1830 it had reached 1,000 million. But while it took about a million years to reach this figure, it took only another century to double, and in the short span of thirty years, the total of 3,000 million was reached, in 1960.

At the current rate of increase, short of some global holocaust or the advent of a miraculous birth control drug or device, the world might well have more than 7,000 million people by AD 2000—less than thirty years away and within the lifetime of the majority of people already on this planet.

While this world population explosion is a grim reality, there is no such thing as a single *world* population problem. To different nations and regions this population growth poses problems of varying

[1] For a detailed examination of India's population problems see S. Chandrasekhar, *Infant Mortality, Population Growth and Family Planning in India* (London, Allen & Unwin and Chapel Hill; University of North Carolina Press, 1972).

magnitude. And to present-day India, population growth is a real and serious threat to her overall economic and social advancement, indeed to her very survival.

INDIA'S POPULATION GROWTH: 1871–1971

The growth of India's population from the earliest times to the present, from available evidence, is not unlike the growth of world population over long stretches of time. The population grew very slowly or remained stationary over most of her history and began to increase rapidly only during the last half-century.

Table 3 summarizes the growth of India's population during the last hundred years. During the first fifty years of India's census history, 1871–1921 (the first census was taken in 1871–2), India's population increased by about 60 million. But during the second half of the century (1921–71), the population increased by 296 million. The year 1921 proved to be a great divide, when the nation began slowly to control famines and epidemics. The result has been not only a great multiplication; the multiplication itself has been going on at an accelerating rate.

Table 3. Growth of India's Population, 1872–1971

Census year	Population adjusted to the present area (in millions)	Increase or decrease (in millions)	Percentage variation during the preceding decade
1871–1872	190·0	—	—
1881	206·0	16·0	8·37
1891	236·7	30·7	14·88
1901	236·3	−0·4	−0·20
1911	252·1	15·8	5·73
1921	251·4	−0·7	−0·31
		(61·4)	(32·32)
1931	279·0	27·6	11·01
1941	316·7	37·7	14·22
1951	361·1	44·4	13·31
1961	439·2	78·1	21·50
1971	547·9	108·7	24·80
		(295·5)	(117·54)

India today is literally experiencing a population explosion, thanks to the fragmentary but slowly growing benefits of the health revolution. The birth rate has remained nearly constant at 40–38 per 1,000, whereas the death rate has registered a definitive decline, to about 15 per 1,000 in 1971. More children survive; more people grow older; and the expectation of life at birth, which was 23 in 1931, has increased to 55 in 1971. During the post-independence period (1947–71), India has added more than 200 million to her population, an addition roughly equivalent to the total United States population in 1970.

REASONS FOR GROWTH

What are the factors behind the great increase in numbers during the last half-century? To begin with, India already had a large population, and even a small and nominal rate of increase would have yielded an impressive addition decade after decade.

Second, a part of the explanation is to be found in India's formerly relatively high birth rates and recently rapidly declining death rates. These in themselves are products of the nation's age and sex composition. India has a young population: according to the 1961 census, 40·2 per cent of the total population was in the 0–14 age group, 47·9 per cent aged 15–49, and 11·9 per cent 50 and over. (The 1971 census data will not be available for another two years.) Thus young and more fecund people predominate in the population. If all these young people marry, as they are bound to do in view of the universality of the married state in India, the population is bound to increase at an even higher rate than it has in the past.

Third, this well-known feature of the universality of the married state in India, documented in the census reports during the last hundred years, reveals that almost everyone in India, sooner or later, usually sooner, gets married. Marriage is not merely a social institution; it is a quasi-religious duty. As an individual's economic security or emotional maturity are seldom a prerequisite, and as there is no individual choice, by and large, in obtaining a husband or wife, there is no economic or emotional deterrent to marriage. Bachelors and spinsters are therefore rare in India, and nearly every adult male and female participates in reproduction.

Fourth, early marriages are still the rule in India, although child marriages have virtually disappeared. But though forty-two years have elapsed since the Child Marriage Restraint Act (the Sarda Act) was passed in 1929, and though the age of consent for girls was raised from 14 in 1929 to 15 in 1956 in the Hindu Code legislation, millions of girls still marry earlier. According to the 1961 census enumeration (the latest age data available), nearly 80 per cent of all young teenagers in the rural areas are married. It has been estimated that the mean age at marriage of Indian females of all caste and religious groups has increased from 13 to 16 in this century.

Fifth, some relief from population pressure was obtained in the past from the traditional if obscurantist feature of the Hindu social scene—the social (not legal) ban on the remarriage of widows. During the last decade, there were some 30 million widows of all ages (including 'virgin widows' who were really widowed, pre-puberty brides), who normally do not marry. But India is fast changing, and of late an increasing number of men, both bachelors and widowers, are willing to marry eligible and unencumbered widows. This welcome negation of the traditional custom of banning the remarriage of widows and withdrawing these women from participating in reproduction contributes its small share to the population problem. In the years to come it is possible that this 'social infertility' may disappear altogether from Indian society.

Sixth, as long as India continues to be predominantly an agrarian economy based on traditional unmechanized subsistence agriculture, with only small beginnings of modernization through the so-called green revolution, the need for a large rural labour force will continue to exist. This need is largely responsible for the desire for sons which has become through the centuries a fixed social and cultural attitude. Further, the fact that there are no old age or retirement benefits or any kind of social security for the vast agricultural population bolsters the strong desire for sons to succeed to the farmstead and support their parents in their old age.

And lastly there is the beginning of the health revolution in India. Perhaps the major decisive factor behind the growth of India's population is the decline in the nation's death rate. The estimated death rate shows a steady decline from 42·6 per 1,000 in 1901 to 15 in 1970. Even more revealing is the decline in the infant mortality rate, from 232 to about 100 for the same period. The maternal and child mortality rates have similarly declined during the last half-century. And the last decade has witnessed a greater decline in the overall death rate than in the entire preceding half-century.

This dramatic and definitive decline in the death rate has been brought about by the Government's action in various directions: an increase in the number of medical colleges (from 20 in 1947 to 95 in 1971) and related institutions, and a consequent increase in trained medical and para-medical personnel; DDT spraying for malaria eradication; BCG vaccination for tuberculosis; the services of trained midwives; the spread of a modicum of health education and services in remote areas; American technical aid, particularly in malaria eradication; and the overall assistance of the World Health Organization and the Colombo Plan.

The near-successful attack on such diseases as malaria and tuberculosis has a kind of cumulative effect which has not been adequately studied in the developing countries. For example, malaria not only kills but leaves those victims who do not succumb debilitated, unproductive and an easy prey to numerous infections. Therefore malaria eradication not only lowers the death rate, but raises the individual's overall resistance to disease; and what is more, indirectly increases the birth rate. In response to all this, not only has the general death rate declined but the expectation of life at birth has increased from 23 years in 1931 to 55 in 1971, leading eventually to a rise in the birth rate.

Another factor of considerable importance responsible for India's population growth is governmental and political stability in India. The transfer of political power from Britain to India has been relatively smooth, reflecting credit on both sides. And the political evolution during the last quarter of a century has revealed both the adaptability of Indian political leadership to modern democratic and parliamentary institutions and the resilience of the Indian constitution. While sporadic riots and minor regional revolts have not been wanting, India has been spared the bloodly upheavals of both military dictatorships and running civil wars that some surrounding Asian countries have had to endure after their political liberation.

INDIA'S BIRTH AND DEATH RATES

A major difficulty in Indian demography is that of under-registration of births and deaths, the magnitude of which varies between state and state, city and village. Birth and death rates derived from registered vital statistics are highly misleading. The only reliable figures come from the decennial censuses.

During the decade 1951–61 the intercensal increase in population was 78·1 million and the decennial rate of increase was 1·95. On the basis of this increase the birth rates for the decade were estimated to range between 44 and 40 per 1,000 and the death rate between 24·5 and 20·5.

On the basis of these estimates the decade 1961–71 was expected to add about 122 million to the 1961 census total of 439·2 million, which was expected to reach 561 million by 1971. The assumption was that the birth rate was around 40 per 1,000 and the death rate around 16 per 1,000, resulting in a 2·4 per cent increase. This, translated into round numbers, meant that there were about 21 million births a year, some 8 million deaths, resulting in a net annual addition of 13 million. This was the favoured projection of the expert committee of the Indian Government's Planning Commission.

But the 1971 census population total, announced on 1 April, was, as pointed out earlier, 547 million. While this represents more than 108 million over the 1961 census total, and a 24·8 per cent increase over the last decade, it also fell short by 14 million of the Government projection. The average annual exponential growth rate for this decade is 2·20 per cent per annum, which is significantly lower than what was expected (2·5 per cent). While under-enumeration of population in a census is always a problem, it is unlikely (beyond a few million) that the 1971 census suffered any more in this respect than did the 1961 census.

The increase in the exponential annual growth rate for the decade 1961–71 (2·20 per cent) over that for the decade 1951–61 (1·95 per cent) shows that mortality rates are still falling. This change in growth would be achieved by a drop in mortality of 2½ points from an estimated mortality of 22·8 for 1951–61 to 20·3 for 1961–71. This drop in mortality is small but other indications are that the crude mortality rate could have dropped to 15 per 1,000. If this is the case, as is likely, then to achieve the growth rate of 2·20 per cent for 1961–71, the birth rates would have also had to drop by 4 or more points. This is illustrated in Table 4 where growth rates for 1951–61 and 1961–71 are compared with possible birth and death rates which could give rise to these growth rates.

Table 4. Possible Birth and Death Rates which may Account for Decennial Growth Rates

1951–1961 Growth rate = 1·95		1961–1971 Growth rate = 2·20	
Birth rate	Death rate	Birth rate	Death rate
44	24·5	44	22
43	23·5	42	20
42	22·5	40	18
41	21·5	38	16
40	20·5	36	14

On the assumption that death rates have dropped at least 6 points, birth rates would have dropped 4 points or less. Since death rates have probably dropped more than 2½ points, it is reasonable to conclude tentatively that birth rates are also declining. The widespread provision of family planning services to Indian couples (to be described shortly) could well have facilitated this decline. Indeed, if this is so, the impact of the family planning services may be even greater than it appears, since the beginning of the really intensive family planning campaign dates only from early 1967 and took some time to gain momentum. The 1971 census total, lower than what was projected, could well reflect the beginnings of a decline in the birth rate as a result of the last five years of the family planning campaign.

THE PROBLEM

In today's world, India ranks second in population numbers (the People's Republic of China heads the list with more than 800 million people) and seventh in land area. That is, with only 2·4 per cent of the world's total land area, India has to support about 14 per cent of the world's total population, while this population enjoys – if that is the correct word – no more than 1·5 per cent of the total world income. In a word, India's population problem is one of grim poverty, the product of limited land area and even more limited resources and technological know-how.

India's rapid population growth is manifestly central to her economic and social development. Her population growth is problematic in at least three major areas. As the available agricultural land is already densely settled a further increase in population pressure does not add to agricultural productivity. Even while some potentially productive land may be available in some areas, additional population increases would hardly yield increased food production, for want of capital equipment and scientific agricultural techniques.

Secondly, the considerable net annual addition to the population implies that a larger share of each year's income is invested in maintaining the population at the existing low level of living. The larger the investment, the smaller the share of annual income available to raise the per capita current consumption.

Lastly the high birth rates in an already young population, referred to earlier, create a heavy load of dependent children on the working population. Supporting numerous children puts an intolerable burden on the workers who in any case find it hard to save and invest for family betterment or overall economic development.

All these difficulties are reflected in various indices of the nation's economic growth. To cite only two crucial ones: India's total national income increased from Rs 86 thousand million in 1948–9 to 149 thousand million in 1968–9, or an increase of 73·25 per cent over two decades. But the per capita income increased during the same period from Rs 249 to Rs 300—a meagre 19·76 per cent. Not only is India's per capita income today among the lowest in the world, but the rate of increase over two decades of national development is remarkably insignificant.

The growth of India's population must be viewed against the nation's total food production and the per capita consumption. India has been attempting through all her four Five Year Plans to bring more land under the plough and to make the cultivated land yield more. The total production of food grains in India increased from about 50 million tons in 1950–51 to about 96 million tons in 1967–8 and 107·8 million tons in 1970–1. Despite this improvement the gap between the total amount of food production and actual needs to meet minimum nutritional requirements is wider than ever before. While the net availability of food grains increased by 43 per cent between 1951 and 1967, the per capita net availability of food grains increased by 2 per cent. The growth of India's population is a major obstacle to raising the per capita food consumption.

In view of these difficulties, a detailed anti-natalist policy for India was formulated in the beginning of 1967 by the present writer with the major objective of reducing the nation's birth rate of 41 per 1,000 to 25 per 1,000 as expeditiously as possible, through a wide variety of family planning and population control measures.

HOW INDIA IS TACKLING HER HIGH BIRTH RATE

Though a nominal policy promoting family planning has been in existence since the beginning of the First Five Year Plan in 1951, it was only in early 1967 after the new government headed by Mrs Indira Gandhi came into power that a vigorous, new, anti-natalist policy was formulated and an all-out campaign to control population growth launched.

The population policy of promoting smaller families (two or three children at most per family) has to be made effective within the framework of an ancient but open society wedded to a modern democratic form of government. The need for the small family norm had to be brought home to nearly 100 million couples (in a 70 per cent illiterate population) living in some 564,000 far-flung villages and 2,700 towns and cities, using some 14 major languages and more than 200 dialects.

The available mass media—newspapers and periodicals, the cinema, All-India Radio, as well as talks and dialogues, group discussions, plays and skits, bill boards, puppetry and religious discourses—all have been pressed into use to carry the slogans 'Two or three children—enough', or 'If you have two, that will do', with the Red Triangle symbol to identify the programmes and location of family planning clinics, supplies and services.

While in a country like India radio should be the most effective instrument for our propaganda (in fact, the present writer once proposed the gift of a transistor set as an incentive to any father of three children willing to undergo vasectomy), radios are too expensive for the average villager; and the community (radio) sets presented to about a quarter of the village *panchayats* by the Government are frequently out of order. (Repairing a radio set in a village is not an easy task.)

ABORTION IN A CROWDED WORLD

Though India is the second largest film-producing country in the world, family planning as a subject has received little attention from commercial film producers. But by means of attractive offers the Government of India has encouraged the production of family planning films by professional and amateur movie makers. The Government itself has produced films on the subject in most of the regional languages and released them through the country's 6,050 cinemas—but all of them reach only about 25 per cent of the country's population.

In a predominantly illiterate country, perhaps television would be the real answer to the mass dissemination of family planning knowledge, but unfortunately India has only one experimental station in New Delhi with a thirty-mile radius.

METHODS OF FAMILY PLANNING

In a poor and technologically backward country the choice of an ideal contraceptive poses numerous problems. Further, in a vast culturally heterogeneous population (ranging from a Nobel Prize winner to an illiterate tribal peasant who may not connect coitus with conception), no single method can be suitable to all.

Hence 'the cafeteria approach' where theoretically all the scientifically approved contraceptives and services are made available free to the people in the Government hospitals and family planning clinics, but for mass consumption only three methods are now advocated: sterilization (vasectomy for fathers and tubectomy for mothers), IUDs and condoms. (The pill has been approved for select groups of wives in a pilot project.)

What have the accomplishments been so far? Up to the beginning of 1973 some 13 million persons had been sterilized. About 82 per cent of these sterilizations are vasectomies and the rest are tubectomies. They are not all urban cases; the rural population has contributed substantially to these figures. An interesting feature of sterilization is that recently tubectomies have become more popular than vasectomies. Though tubectomy, compared to vasectomy, is a relatively major surgical procedure and more expensive, the fact that it is preferred shows that women are becoming increasingly aware of the problem and want to solve it without waiting for their husbands to decide on vasectomy.

As for IUD, so far some 4·5 million loops have been inserted. But the method introduced in India in 1965 has not proved popular because of excessive bleeding and intra-menstrual spotting in about 15 per cent of the cases and involuntary expulsion in about 6 per cent. The real problem is the lack of sufficient numbers of dedicated women physicians who are willing to work in rural areas and spend some time in pre-insertion talks and post-insertion follow-up of their patients.

And last is the condom or sheath. The total requirement is about 300 million pieces and with the setting up of a Government owned factory, Hindustan Latex Ltd in Trivandrum, the shortage of sheaths has been solved. The Government has launched vigorous promotion campaigns, and once the demand is created the simple device may become as popular in the Indian countryside as it has in the rest of the world.

CLINICS, HOSPITALS AND MEDICAL PERSONNEL

All these family planning methods and necessary supplies and advice are available in both urban and rural centres, and in addition there are some mobile units. In 1970 there were 3,687 urban family planning clinics (1,022 run by state governments; 368 by local bodies; 371 by voluntary organizations; and 1,926 by other urban institutions doing family planning work). More important, there were in the same year 41,151 modest family planning centres in the rural areas. (These include 4,812 main rural family planning centres, 28,912 sub-centres, and 7,427 other rural medical and para-medical institutions.) Besides these, some 862 mobile units for inserting IUDs and performing sterilizations are functioning.

While the Government of India is taking the necessary steps to provide men and women doctors for these centres, the paucity of doctors, particularly women doctors trained in family planning and willing to work in rural areas, continues to be an acute problem. In fact, India, like all developing countries, is faced with the perennial problem of finding trained workers at all levels, whether nurses, midwives, health educators or health visitors. (And yet there are about 4,000 Indian doctors trained in India but working in the United Kingdom, Canada, the United States and elsewhere in the world.) But by special scholarships to medical students who opt to work in family planning, and special emoluments for doctors working in rural hardship posts, India is trying to meet this difficulty.

Finally, the Government has brought private workers into the nation's official family planning programme at various levels. Till 1967, family planning work was confined to doctors on the Government's payroll. Some 35,000 private medical practitioners, who naturally charge a fee for advice, supplies and services, were not brought into the Government programme. The result was a latent hostility on their part to the official programme which gave everything free in Government hospitals. Now the private physicians and surgeons work for the programme on the basis of a mutually agreed payment.

The practitioners of the ancient indigenous systems of Indian medicine – *Ayurveda, Siddha* and *Unani* – who cater to the simple medical needs of the rural population, have also been brought into the programme. Besides these, the Government has enlisted the support of such diverse groups as various political parties, women's organizations, social workers, foreign Christian (Catholic and Protestant) missionary hospitals and doctors, business and industrial leaders, labour unions, various religious organizations, municipalities, *Panchayati Raj* and other elected agencies, and Gandhian workers. These efforts have given family planning programmes real national support from a wide spectrum of voluntary agencies.

These are the major features of India's current programme to cut down her birth rate.

RAISING THE AGE OF CONSENT

While the term 'age of consent' is not a legal one it is generally used to denote the age below which a person cannot validly give his or her consent to certain acts. Thus a girl below sixteen years of age is not legally capable of giving her consent for sexual intercourse, according to the Indian Penal Code Amendment Act XLII of 1949. In this context the 'age of consent' may be said to be the attainment of sixteen years of age.

A proposal which will help reduce the country's total fertility is to raise the age of consent for girls and boys. As responsible and disciplined children are raised in homes where parents are mature and responsible citizens themselves, the Government hopes to raise the age of consent to eighteen for girls and twenty for boys. Raising the minimum age of marriage is inherently desirable to improve the social climate in India, quite apart from its beneficent effects on population growth.

It has been established that either as a result of being generally more mature, or because of greater opportunities for education and training and chances of gainful employment, or a combination of these, girls marrying at a later age favour and adopt family planning measures much more readily. Marrying at a slightly higher age cuts down the reproductive span and some recent studies show that if the minimum age at marriage for females were fixed at twenty years, the reduction in total fertility would range from 12 to 25 per cent. Fertility is affected by a number of biological and institutional factors, of which the age at marriage is an important one. In any case, there is no doubt that by marrying a few years later, after they have had the opportunity at least to complete their high school education and obtain some gainful employment, young women would be better equipped to embark upon marriage and parenthood with a greater degree of mature responsibility.

The age at which young men marry has been slowly going up to twenty and twenty-one years, particularly in urban areas, owing to possibilities of extended education, economic necessity, housing shortages, and other factors. However, in rural areas, the concept of late marriage has not spread. If the villages were provided with some new vocational high schools for girls with emphasis on home economics, hygiene and mother-craft, the girls could be kept busy, and this might help to postpone marriage by a few years. But only when the necessary social climate is created and rural parents are convinced of the gains of education and the benefit of later marriages, can legislation on this subject be successfully enforced.

AREAS OF IGNORANCE

An overall review of the entire Indian family planning programme during the last five years reveals that there are still three large areas where we are groping for correct answers and workable solutions. They are in the fields of motivation, communication, and finding an ideal contraceptive for substandard circumstances. There is a pressing need for initiating high-powered research to find permanent answers to these three baffling problems.

The first is *motivation*. How does one motivate an average husband or wife or a couple in the milieu of rural poverty or an urban slum to want family planning? How do we explain to an average illiterate couple resigned to a parody of living on a pavement 'dwelling' that a large family is utterly incompatible with a higher standard of living? How does one convince them that one of the solutions to family poverty is to have fewer children? In the Indian context of low incomes, if one wants a better home, more and better food, adequate clothing, educational and medical facilities, then it is obvious that one should not have more than one or two children. This statement seems so simple, so obvious. But when one goes to a slum or tries to convince a pavement dweller that he should postpone marriage, and that when he does marry he should not have more than one or two children, the invariable reaction is an adverse one. Obviously, talking about the world's population explosion or India's population problem and the shortage of resources is irrelevant. But even the problem of poverty at the most basic personal individual or family level does not seem to help. The fatalistic resignation to impoverishment appears to be complete.

Obviously incentives can play some part. The present controversy is between money incentives versus service incentives. Unfortunately, no serious scientific study of the role of incentives in motivating citizens to adopt a particular course of action has been made in India. It is not known for certain what kind of incentives will best promote the adoption of family planning under Indian conditions. Some consider any incentive a bribe. Is it? These questions demand careful study and considered answers if some significant progress is to be made in helping poor couples who desperately need small families to accept voluntary family planning services.

The second problem is that of *communication*. In the ordinary sense, communication is extremely poor and all the existing channels of mass media do not reach more than 25 per cent of the country's population. Predominant illiteracy (according to the 1971 census only 29·35 per cent of the people were found literate) is a barrier to the effectiveness of the printed word and, as observed already, the radio is too expensive for most of the rural population. Even the cinema, which is so popular in our urban areas as an escape mechanism, has not become a permanent feature of Indian rural life.

The third and last problem is the desperate need for *an ideal contraceptive*. Almost all the research on contraceptives, mechanical, chemical, surgical and oral, is carried on in the West—the United States, the United Kingdom and Europe. Western scientists have in mind, by and large, the problems posed in advanced countries. While human physiology is the same the world over, the economic, social and psychological conditions under which human beings function vary enormously between country and country, between city and village, and between regions within the same country.

In the advanced and industrialized West, even in relatively poor communities, bathrooms of some kind, running water, privacy, electricity, a chemist's shop, the availability of a doctor or a nurse or some para-medical personnel, a clinical consultation, at least quasi-literacy, a little knowledge of human reproduction—for the most part all are taken for granted. But this is not so in rural India which accounts for 80 per cent of the nation's population. Hence the need for an ideal contraceptive from the point of view of India's backward conditions.

CONCLUSION

Wonderful as the green revolution is, it will not by itself solve the problems posed by excessive fertility. Man does not live by bread alone but by other goods and services as well. The battle against hunger may be won but the war against poverty lost. Hence the need to wage war on two fronts: increasing the production of food and other commodities and services and, equally important, vigorously campaigning to cut down the nation's birth rate.

As India is exploring all available means to cut down her birth rate, the question of liberalizing the present restrictive Indian law on abortion has to be considered. The legalization of abortion in the Indian context would be both a health and a demographic measure. It has been estimated that some 5 million induced abortions a year, all technically illegal, take place in India in unhygienic and insanitary 'back street clinics'. Every year thousands of women face mutilation or death in the hands of these unqualified abortionists. The legalization of abortion would be both a death control and a birth control measure: death control in the sense that those who want abortion could obtain a safe one from a qualified surgeon in an approved clinic or hospital under aseptic conditions; birth control since as there appears to be a direct correlation between abortion and a declining birth rate, this measure would serve as another family planning method, particularly in cases where conventional contraceptive methods have failed, and contribute its share to solving the problem of the high rate of population growth in India. Contraception is certainly preferable to abortion. There is no doubt that prevention is always better than cure, but cure, when possible, should never be denied.

Chapter 3

India Liberalizes her Abortion Law

THE CHANGING CLIMATE

A little more than a century ago abortion in India was made a crime for which the mother as well as the abortionist could be punished in all cases except where the abortion had to be induced in order to save the life of the mother. This very strict law has been observed in the breach in a considerable number of cases in rural and urban areas all over India. Whatever the ethical and moral feelings professed by society as a whole on the question of induced abortion, it is an incontrovertible fact that a large number of mothers are prepared to risk their lives in an illegal abortion rather than carry that particular child to term.

Furthermore, a great majority of these pregnant women are married, and have no particular need to conceal their pregnancy. In recent years, as health services have expanded and hospital facilities have been used to the fullest extent by all classes of society, doctors have been confronted all too often with gravely ill or dying (pregnant) women who have tampered with their uterus with a view to causing an abortion and, while not fully succeeding in their purpose, have suffered miserable and severe consequences. An abortion which could have been aseptically performed under proper medical supervision becomes under these circumstances a case where doctors have to fight, sometimes in vain, for the life of the mother, expending the best available skill, drugs and equipment. It was this sheer futile wastage of precious human lives, the loss of countless mothers, that made the medical profession and the general public demand that the question of illegal abortion be reviewed and re-examined as a whole.

A law that rigidly prohibits something that nevertheless continues as a fairly widespread practice in the community is one that requires re-examination and, if necessary, change. Law is the vehicle of society. Therefore the question of how far permitted abortions can serve the wider purposes of family and society can bear dispassionate examination. The family as a unit of society has always been safeguarded and even hedged in by customs and conventions, rules and regulations based on ethical, moral and religious values. Besides, society is not a static but a changing and evolving entity, and the family pattern changes with it.

The India of today bears witness to changes which are unconventional and even radical. The whole process of economic development, involving rapid and large-scale industrialization and technological change, is rapidly ushering in a new way of life affecting not only the economic and political but also the social spheres of life.

It would not be wise, even if it were possible, to utilize modern science and technology for the economic betterment of our people and yet preserve unchanged the traditional pattern of family organization and life. The remarkably changed position of women and children in the new society that is being built up is a very relevant factor, for these vulnerable groups cannot be regarded any longer or in any manner as subordinate with lesser rights. The equality of sexes is enshrined in India's constitution and is being built into the foundations of modern society. The standards of care and nurture of our children are far advanced today compared with conditions some fifty or even twenty-five years ago; and the importance of the welfare of our children as future citizens of the country is too obvious to need any special emphasis. Hence the need for a careful review and a new appraisal of our existing attitudes and laws on abortion became imperative.

THE ABORTION STUDY COMMITTEE AND ITS RECOMMENDATIONS

The Central Family Planning Board of the Government of India – a policy-making body – at a meeting held on 25 August 1964 expressed some concern over the problem of abortion and recommended the appointment of a committee to examine the subject of abortion in all its aspects, legal, medical, moral and social, and to make suitable suggestions to alter the existing law on the subject.

The Ministry of Health and Family Planning of the Government of India appointed an eleven-member Committee on 29 September 1964 with Mr Shantilal Shah, then Health Minister of Maharashtra State, as its chairman, to study the question of legalization of abortion. The Committee deliberated on this subject for a little more than two years and submitted their recommendations in December 1966.

The Abortion Study Committee, for their own information and as a prelude to their recommendations, carried out a few studies. One consisted of a fairly full compilation of available data on trends in abortion in various countries of the world, the proportion of abortions to live births, morbidity and mortality rates for legal and illegal abortions, and their numbers and ratio among the married and the unmarried. In addition, some data on the incidence of induced abortion and its cost were collected. The question of abortion in India was studied against the background of the available international picture.

Another study was conducted to elicit the reactions of various important persons, leaders of opinions and heads of medical and other institutions. A specially devised questionnaire (see Appendix 3) was sent to interested and responsible persons in the various Ministries of the Government of India, the State Governments, the members of the Planning Commission, Members of Parliament and State Legislative Assemblies. The members of the Central and State (Government) Family Planning Boards and many interested legal, medical, political, social and religious organizations were also invited to respond.

The questionnaire elicited responses from 570 individuals and organizations, mainly health and medical officers (127), private physicians (235), and voluntary welfare associations including planned parenthood and women's groups (140). A great majority (96 per cent) of the respondents favoured a legal abortion to save a mother's life or to ensure her physical and mental health, 82 per cent in cases of rape, while more than a half (57 per cent) favoured abortion for socio-economic reasons. The welfare organizations which represented the poor took a more liberal position than that taken by the medical, legal and other organized professional groups.

The Committee also interviewed selected individuals from a cross-section of Indian public life in cities such as Bombay, Delhi, Calcutta and Madras. In addition, it had the benefit of several articles on the subject in the popular and professional press as well as the wide spectrum of public opinion reflected in readers' letters to the daily press on the question of the liberalization of abortion laws in India.

The Committee submitted its report to the Government at the end of 1966. The Report offered the following recommendations:

4·1 The abortion law in India at present is as follows:

> Indian Penal Code. Section 312. 'Whoever voluntarily causes a woman with child to miscarry shall, if such miscarriage be not caused in good faith for the purpose of saving the life of the woman, be punished with imprisonment of either description for a term which may extend to three years or with fine or with both; and if the woman be quick with child, shall be punished with imprisonment either description for a term which may extend to seven years and shall also be liable to fine.'
>
> *Explanation*: A woman who causes herself to miscarry is within the meaning of this section.
>
> The word 'miscarriage' used in the section includes not only abortions

but also expulsion of viable foetus before the normal birth. The only exception is in case of a miscarriage caused in good faith for the purpose of saving the life of the mother.

4.2 (i) The Committee considers the above provision too restrictive; and therefore recommends that it should be liberalized to allow termination of pregnancy by a qualified medical practitioner acting in good faith not only for saving the pregnant woman's life but also:

- a. When the continuance of the pregnancy would involve serious risk to the life, or grave injury to the health, whether physical or mental, of the pregnant woman, whether before, at, or after the birth; or
- b. When there is a substantial risk that if the child were born it would suffer from such physical or mental abnormalities as to be seriously handicapped in life; or
- c. When the pregnancy results from rape, intercourse with an unmarried girl under the age of sixteen or intercourse with a mentally defective woman.

(ii) The Committee further recommends that the following conditions be complied with in connection with any treatment for the termination of a pregnancy, that is to say:

- a. Abortions authorized under the above recommendation can be performed only by a person who holds a qualification granted by an authority specified or notified in any of the schedules to the Indian Medical Council Act 1956 (202 of 1956), as modified up to the 1st December, 1964.
- b. The treatment must be carried out in a place for the time being approved for the purpose, by the Government of India or State Government.
- c. The opinion must be certified in writing by the practitioner who carries out the termination of pregnancy before the treatment is begun.
- d. There has been before treatment a consent in writing by the pregnant woman, or, if under eighteen years of age, the pregnant girl and one of her parents or of the pregnant girl and her guardian for the termination of the pregnancy.

Provided that where the practitioner is of the opinion, formed in good faith, that the termination is immediately necessary in order to save the life of the pregnant woman (and certifies his opinion in writing either before or after carrying out the treatment) conditions (b) and (d) need not be complied with.

(iii) The Government should prescribe rules requiring the qualified medical practitioner who terminates a pregnancy to give notice of the termination, and such other information relating to the termination as may be prescribed by the regulations within such period as may be prescribed; and with respect to the disposal of certificates.

The information so furnished shall not be made public or divulged to any person other than a police officer especially authorized to obtain such information or under order of a Court of Law.

4.3 The Committee had the opportunity to see a Draft Medical Termination of Pregnancy Bill recently discussed in the British Parliament and has utilized its provisions in making the above recommendations.

4.4. The Committee is aware that it may be difficult to distinguish genuine from non-genuine cases. The Committee, however, feels that the likelihood of a few non-genuine cases should not prevent protection to a large number of genuine cases.

4.5 The Committee while making the above recommendations also strongly recommends that:

    a. In order to prevent the danger of repeated abortions in the case of women who are not fit to bear the strain of further pregnancies the medical practitioner should advise the woman and/or her husband to undergo voluntary sterilization.

    b. The idea of a small family norm achieved through control of conception should be vigorously promoted.

    c. Readily accessible services for family planning should be extended.

    d. Family Life Education to develop healthy and responsible attitudes towards sex, marriage and parenthood should be promoted.

4.6 There is very little statistical and other material available in India on this highly controversial subject of induced abortion. It has attracted public attention only recently. The Committee is aware that its recommendations are likely to be criticized either as falling too short or as going too far according to the critic's attitude. Nevertheless it is of the view that they should be placed before the Government for their consideration as it feels that the recommendations are practicable and necessary under present conditions.[1]

THE CENTRAL FAMILY PLANNING COUNCIL'S RECOMMENDATIONS

The Central Family Planning Council (the policy-making body of the Ministry of Health and Family Planning, Government of India), composed of the Health Ministers of all the seventeen States of the Union and comparable officers of the eleven Union Territories, besides representatives of various concerned voluntary organizations,

---

[1] *Report of the Committee to Study the Question of Legalization of Abortion*, chap. 4, Recommendations (New Delhi, Ministry of Health and Family Planning, 1966), pp. 51–4.

in their meeting held on 7 October 1967, under the chairmanship of Dr S. Chandrasekhar, India's Minister for Health and Family Planning, recommended the acceptance of the recommendations of the Committee as amended below:

The Committee considers the above (Section 312 IPC) provision too restrictive and, therefore, recommends that it should be liberalized to allow termination of pregnancy by a qualified medical practitioner acting in good faith not only for saving the pregnant woman's life but also:

a. When the continuance of the pregnancy would involve serious risk to the life, or grave injury to the health, whether physical or mental, of the pregnant woman, whether before, at, or after the birth; or

b. Provided the woman or her husband undergo voluntary sterilization to ward off the danger of repeated abortions and further pregnancies except in cases where under exceptional circumstances such sterilization is not considered necessary by the authorized medical practitioner carrying out the termination of pregnancy.

Illustration

a. If a couple has been using family planning devices for the purposes of planning their family, and if a pregnancy occurs as a result of failure of such devices, the anguish arising from continuance of such an unwanted pregnancy may constitute a grave injury to the mental health of the pregnant woman.

b. When there is a substantial risk that if the child were born it would suffer from such physical or mental abnormalities as to be seriously handicapped in life; or

c. When the pregnancy results from rape, intercourse with an unmarried girl under the age of 16 or intercourse with a mentally defective woman.

The Committee further recommends that the following conditions be complied with in connection with any treatment for the termination of a pregnancy, that is to say:

a. Abortion authorized under the aforesaid recommendations is performed, when the duration of pregnancy extends up to three months, by a person (hereinafter referred to as qualified medical practitioner) who holds a qualification granted by an authority specified or notified in any of the Schedules of the Indian Medical Council Act, 1956 (202 of 1956) as notified from time to time and is registered either with the Medical Council of India or one of the State Medical Councils.

Where the period of pregnancy exceeds three months, such an abortion is performed by the qualified medical practitioner only after obtaining a second opinion in the matter from another qualified medical practitioner.

b. The treatment must be carried out in a place for the time being approved for the purpose, by the Government of India or State Government.

c. The opinion and the second opinion, as the case may be, must be certified in writing by the practitioner who carried out the termination of pregnancy before the treatment is begun.

d. There has been before treatment a consent in writing by the pregnant woman, or, if under eighteen years of age, the pregnant girl and one of her parents or of the pregnant girl and her guardian for the termination of the pregnancy.

Provided that where the practitioner is of the opinion, formed in good faith, that the termination is immediately necessary in order to save the life of the pregnant woman (and certifies his opinion in writing either before or after carrying out the treatment) conditions (b) and (d) need not be complied with. The Government should prescribe rules requiring the qualified medical practitioner who terminates the pregnancy to give notice of the termination and such other information relating to the termination as may be prescribed by the regulations within such period as may be prescribed, and with respect to the disposal of certificates. The information so furnished shall not be made public or divulged to any person except as required by law.

HISTORY OF THE CURRENT LIBERAL LEGISLATION

As a result of joint consultations between the Ministry of Health and Family Planning and the Ministry of Law, the following Draft Bill, entitled 'The Medical Termination of Pregnancy Bill, 1969', was finalized. This measure received considerable assistance from Mr Panampalli Govinda Menon, then Union Law Minister, now unfortunately deceased, and officials of the Law Ministry. The Bill incorporated some suggestions received from the various State Governments. The Bill as presented in these pages was approved by all but one of the State Governments and those of the Union Territories of the Indian Union. It was introduced by the present writer in the Rajya Sabha (Upper House) of the Indian Parliament on 17 November 1969.

While introducing the Bill the writer sought support for it on the grounds that it was primarily a health measure. While the demographic factor was played down for obvious reasons, the health aspect was important in that legal hospital abortions would greatly reduce the morbidity and mortality resulting from illegal, unsanitary, botched-up abortions.

The writer pleaded that the problem of abortion must be examined from three basic points of view in any society, and particularly in an underdeveloped economy like India's.

First, there is the point of view of the woman—her physical and mental health, and her freedom. Apart from the Government's decision to pass this measure, the writer personally believes that any woman in India, at any time, should be able to obtain a legal abortion from a public hospital or a private clinic without giving a reason. This may be a radical position for the present climate in India but it is high time that women became their own masters. In an enlightened world there should be no need for them to suffer from the ageless slavery of unwanted pregnancies. We have come a long way in emancipating our women but their emancipation cannot be complete unless we grant them the right not to have a baby they do not want. Behind the dry statistics of 5 million illegal abortions every year in India (and probably ten times that number in the world) lies an immeasurable mass of human anguish. It is imperative that our society should consider a woman a full human being and not a mere human incubator.

Secondly, we must examine abortion from the point of view of the unborn child who may be physically deformed or mentally retarded, and the unwanted child who becomes the unloved, uncared for, and in time the delinquent child. The problems here are too obvious to need comment, especially in view of the daily newspaper evidence of the growing incidence of delinquent behaviour of children and teenagers.

And lastly, we must examine abortion from the point of view of the state and society and the total socio-economic and demographic picture. The unwanted child who cannot be supported by his parents or even the larger joint family (which is gradually breaking up) ends up on the pavement with a beggar's bowl, and becomes a starving, disgruntled and anti-social citizen, a burden to himself, society and the state. India's poor standard of living and low levels of consumption are being tackled by the Government but there are limits to what a government can do. 'Demographically we are running so fast that economically, despite all the progress made by the Government's three Five Year Plans, we are almost standing still.'[2]

The parliamentary debate revealed a large measure of sympathy with the aims of the Bill as well as some ignorance and hesitation about certain possible abuses of the measure when implemented. What the Government and the present writer wanted was not a mere numerical majority of votes but a near consensus of agreement on the need for this legislation for demographic, health and even eugenic reasons. Therefore, on the suggestion of several senior members of both the ruling Congress party and various opposition parties, the motion for reference of the Bill to the Joint Select Committee composed of members of both Houses of Parliament was moved in the

[2] For the full text of the speech see *India, Rajya Sabha Debates* (1969), pp. 66. Also 'India May Revise Law on Abortion', *New York Times* (23 November 1969).

Rajya Sabha (Upper House) on 3 December 1969 and was adopted by the House on 8 December 1969. The Lok Sabha (Lower House) concurred in the motion on 24 December 1969.

THE ABORTION BILL AS INTRODUCED IN THE RAJYA SABHA ON 17 NOVEMBER 1969

Bill No. 22 of 1969

THE MEDICAL TERMINATION OF PREGNANCY BILL, 1969

A Bill to provide for the termination of certain pregnancies by registered medical practitioners and for matters connected therewith or incidental thereto.

Be it enacted by Parliament in the Twentieth Year of the Republic of India as follows:

1. (i) This Act may be called the Medical Termination of Pregnancy Act, 1969.
   (ii) It extends to the whole of India except the State of Jammu and Kashmir.

2. In this Act, unless the context otherwise requires,
   (a) 'Guardian' means a person having the care of the person of a minor or of his property or of both his person and property;
   (b) 'Lunatic' has the meaning assigned to it in section 3 of the Indian Lunacy Act, 1912 (4 of 1912);
   (c) 'Minor' means a person who, under the provisions of the Indian Majority Act, 1875 (9 of 1875), is to be deemed not to have attained his majority;
   (d) 'Registered medical practitioner' means a medical practitioner who possesses any recognized medical qualification as defined in clause (h) of section 2 of the Indian Medical Council Act, 1956 (102 of 1956), and whose name has been entered in a State Medical Register.

When pregnancies may be terminated by registered medical practitioners:

3. (i) Notwithstanding anything contained in the Indian Penal Code (45 of 1860) a registered medical practitioner shall not be guilty of any offence under that Code or under any other law for the time being in force, if any pregnancy is terminated by him in accordance with the provisions of this Act.
   (ii) Subject to the provisions of sub-section (iv), a pregnancy may be terminated by:
      (a) A registered medical practitioner, where the length of the pregnancy does not exceed twelve weeks, or
      (b) Not less than two registered medical practitioners, acting together, where the length of the pregnancy exceeds twelve weeks, but does not exceed twenty weeks,
   if such medical practitioner is, or such medical practitioners are, as the case may be, of opinion, formed in good faith, that:
      (i) The continuance of the pregnancy would involve a risk to the

life of the pregnant woman or of injury to her physical or mental health; or
(ii) There is a substantial risk that if the child were born, it would suffer from such physical or mental abnormalities as to be seriously handicapped.

Explanation 1: Where any pregnancy is alleged by the pregnant woman to have been caused by rape, the anguish caused by such pregnancy shall be presumed to constitute a grave injury to the mental health of the pregnant woman.

Explanation 2: Where any pregnancy occurs as a result of failure of any device used by any married woman or her husband for the purpose of limiting the number of children, the anguish caused by such unwanted pregnancy may be presumed to constitute a grave injury to the mental health of the pregnant woman.

(iii) In determining whether the continuance of a pregnancy would involve such risk of injury to the health as is mentioned in subsection (ii), account may be taken of the pregnant woman's actual or reasonably foreseeable environment.
(iv) (a) No pregnancy of a married woman shall, if such pregnancy is alleged by such woman to have been caused by rape, be terminated except with the consent in writing of her husband, if he is alive, or of the guardian of her husband, if her husband is a minor or lunatic.
(b) No pregnancy of a widow, who is a minor or lunatic, shall be terminated except with the consent in writing of the guardian of such widow.
(c) No pregnancy of an unmarried girl, who has not attained the age of eighteen years, shall be terminated except with the consent in writing of her father or of her guardian, if her father is not alive.
(d) No pregnancy of an unmarried woman, who, being above the age of eighteen years, is a lunatic, shall be terminated except with the consent in writing of her father or of her guardian, if her father is not alive.
(e) Save as otherwise provided in this sub-section, no pregnancy shall be terminated except with the consent of the pregnant woman.

Place where pregnancy may be terminated:
4. No termination of pregnancy shall be made in accordance with this Act at any place other than:
(a) A hospital established or maintained by Government, or
(b) A place for the time being approved for the purpose of this Act by Government.
5. The provisions of section 4 and so much of the provisions of subsection (ii) of section 3 as relate to the length of the pregnancy and the opinion of not less than two registered medical practitioners, shall not apply to the termination of a pregnancy by a registered

medical practitioner in a case where he is of opinion, formed in good faith, that the termination of such a pregnancy is immediately necessary to save the life, or to save permanent grave injury to the physical or mental health, of the pregnant woman.

Power to make regulations:
6. (i) The State Government may, by regulations:
    (a) Require any such opinion as is referred to in sub-section (ii) of section 3 to be certified by a registered medical practitioner or practitioners concerned, in such form and at such time as may be specified in such regulations, and the preservation or disposal of such certificates;
    (b) Require any registered medical practitioner, who terminates a pregnancy, to give notice of such termination and such other information relating to the termination as may be specified in such regulations;
    (c) Prohibit the disclosure, except to such persons and for such purposes as may be specified in such regulations, of notices given or information furnished in pursuance of such regulations.
   (ii) The notice given and the information furnished in pursuance of regulations made by virtue of clause (b) of sub-section (i) shall be given or furnished, as the case may be, to the Chief Medical Officer of the State.
   (iii) Any person who wilfully contravenes or wilfully fails to comply with the requirements of any regulation made under sub-section (i) shall be liable to be punished with a fine which may extend to one thousand rupees.

Protection of action taken in good faith:
7. No suit or other legal proceedings shall lie against any registered medical practitioner for any damage caused or likely to be caused by anything which is in good faith done or intended to be done under this Act.

STATEMENT OF OBJECTS AND REASONS

The provisions regarding the termination of pregnancy in the Indian Penal Code which were enacted about a century ago were drawn up in keeping with the then British law on the subject. Abortion was made a crime for which the mother as well as the abortionist could be punished except where it had to be induced in order to save the life of the mother. It has been stated that this very strict law has been observed in the breach in a very large number of cases all over the country. Furthermore, most of these mothers are married women, and are under no particular necessity to conceal their pregnancy.

In recent years, when health services have expanded and hospitals are availed of to the fullest extent by all classes of society, doctors have often been confronted with gravely ill or dying pregnant women whose uterus have been tampered with, with a view to causing an abortion and consequently suffered very severely [sic].

There is thus avoidable wastage of the mother's health, strength and, sometimes, life. The proposed measure which seeks to liberalize certain existing provisions relating to termination of pregnancy has been conceived
  (i) As a health measure—when there is danger to the life or risk to the physical or mental health of the woman;
  (ii) On humanitarian grounds—such as when pregnancy arises from a sex crime like rape or intercourse with a lunatic woman etc.;
  (iii) Eugenic grounds—where there is a substantial risk that the child, if born, would suffer from deformities and diseases.

FINANCIAL MEMORANDUM

Clause 4 of the Bill seeks to provide for the termination of certain pregnancies by registered medical practitioners at Government hospitals. If the Bill is enacted, facilities for increased demand will have to be provided by way of vacuum aspirator, increased number of beds, staff, etc. Recurring expenditure of a sum of about Rs 24·00 lakhs (Rs 2,400,000) and a non-recurring expenditure of a sum of about Rs 19·30 lakhs (Rs 1,930,000) is likely to be incurred for providing the said facilities.

MEMORANDUM REGARDING DELEGATED LEGISLATION

Clause 6 of the Bill seeks to empower the State Governments to make regulations:
  (a) Requiring the registered medical practitioners to certify the opinion formed by them in pursuance of sub-clause (ii) of clause 3.
  (b) Specifying the form in which and the time at which such certification shall be furnished and the manner in which such certification shall be preserved and disposed of.
  (c) Requiring any registered medical practitioner who terminates a pregnancy to give notice of such termination and other information relating to such termination to the Chief Medical Officer of the State.
  (d) Prohibiting the disclosure, except to such persons and for such purposes as may be specified by the regulations, of notices or information given by the registered medical practitioners in pursuance of the said regulations.

The matters in relation to which such regulations may be made are matters of detail. The delegation of the legislative power is, therefore, of a normal character.

THE REACTION OF THE STATE AND UNION TERRITORIES' GOVERNMENTS TO THE PROPOSED LEGISLATION

The report (with the recommendations) of the Committee that studied the question of the legalization of abortion was circulated to all the governments of the seventeen States and eleven Union Territories of India to elicit their comments and opinions. The views of the various State Governments have to be taken into consideration before the Central Government can introduce legislation in view of the fact that 'Health' is a State subject in India's Constitution.

The following is a summary of the replies received from the various State and Union Territory Governments:

State or Union Territory

1. Andhra Pradesh — 4.2 (i) (a) Abortion may be restricted to the existing legal limits, i.e. may be permitted if it is done in good faith for the purpose of saving the life of the mother.
4.2 (i) (b). This clause is subject to the condition that the conditions under which abortions could be induced in preventing the birth of a physically handicapped child should be spelled out in detail.
4.2 (i) (c). This clause may be accepted.

2. Assam — The State Government accepts the recommendations.

3. Bihar — The State Government has accepted the recommendations of the Committee *in toto*.

4. Gujarat — The State Government is in general agreement with the various recommendations made.

5. Jammu and Kashmir — Agree in principle to the implementation of the recommendations of the Committee.

6. Haryana — The State Government agrees to the liberalization of abortion law as recommended by the State Committee.

7. Kerala — The State Government is not in a position to support the proposal at present.

8. Madhya Pradesh — The State Government has no comments to offer.

9. Maharashtra — The State Government of Maharashtra accepts the recommendations *in toto*.

10. Mysore — There has been an increasing trend to resort to induced abortion. Since these induced abortions are done without adopting aseptic precautions and without proper medical supervision, the pregnant women are confronted with grave illness or loss of life as a result. The morbidity and mortality among the pregnant women can be reduced considerably if the abortions are performed with proper care by trained doctors.
There have been several instances of women coming to the clinic who have become pregnant

as a result of the failure of a contraceptive method, and requesting medicines to induce abortion. Even after loop insertions it is reported that 2·9 per cent of the women do become pregnant. Many of these women do not wish to have a child and get very disappointed with the method.

Since the cafeteria method has been adopted in this country for family planning, the abortion law should also be liberalized so that those who do not desire to have a child should have the facility of abortion by a trained doctor.

As suggested by the Committee the abortion law has to be liberalized to allow termination of pregnancy by a qualified doctor according to the conditions prescribed by the Committee. This could be done at all major hospitals in the State and the doctors could be trained to perform the induced abortion carefully. These doctors will have to notify the State Family Planning Bureau after each abortion giving the details of the case and the conditions under which the abortion has to be induced. After the abortion the woman should be advised to limit the family by sterilization either on herself or on her husband.

By liberalization of the law regarding induced abortion, the morbidity and mortality among pregnant women could be considerably reduced and at the same time the social stigma against some of the unmarried girls who become pregnant by force could be mitigated.

11. Orissa

The State Government agrees with the recommendations of the Committee. It has, however, suggested that all cases of conception due to rape irrespective of the age or marital status of the woman may be included under items of termination of pregnancy by qualified medical practitioner.

12. Punjab

The report of the Committee on legislation on abortion was considered by the Punjab Government in consultation with the Sub-Committee of the State Family Planning Committee. The comments of the Punjab Government on the report are as follows:

a. *Definition of abortion.* It is necessary while proceeding with any liberalization law relating to abortion that the word 'abortion' be clearly defined. It was decided, therefore, that abortion should be restricted to pregnancies of the duration of twelve weeks or under only.

b. *Scope of liberalization of abortion.* It was decided to suggest to the Central Family Planning Council that abortion should be permitted where certified users of family planning measures report of failure in any of the contraceptive devices they have adopted. This would restore confidence among people in practising family planning.

c. *Limit on abortions.* It was decided to recommend to the Council that if abortion is requested after the third child then it should not be permitted unless either wife or husband undergoes sterilization. This should be a first step before any abortion after the third child is permitted.

d. *Institution of a Local Board.* Abortion should be permitted only under very hygienic conditions in certified hospitals. The Director of Health Services should constitute a Board of experts which should include the Chief Medical Officer and an expert gynaecologist. This Board should carefully scrutinize all cases from the various angles and in conformity with any liberalized law that comes into operation as a result of the acceptance of this report by the Parliament.

e. *Special grants to hospitals.* It is also decided this this Council may be recommended to consider giving special grants to hospitals that take up abortion work.

f. The State Government was of the view that before any liberalized law is enforced relating to abortion intensive training should be given to the doctors so that any such abortions do not expose the patients to very serious risks like the risk of shock, sepsis and incomplete abortion. For this the latest methods, like the suction pump used in European countries and the Soviet Union, should be thoroughly studied to avoid risks of a hasty implementation of liberalized abortion.

g. It was decided to recommend to the Council that the word 'abortion' should be replaced by a more acceptable word. This word has acquired certain undesirable associations.

13. Rajasthan	The State Government agrees with the recommendations of the Committee appointed to study the question of the legalization of abortion.
14. Tamil Nadu	The view of the State Government is similar to that of the Government of Andhra Pradesh.
15. Uttar Pradesh	The State Government accepts the recommendations of the Shantilal Shah Committee subject to the following conditions:

    a. The following clauses of the recommendations should be applicable only to married women;
       (1) When the continuance of the pregnancy involves serious risk to life, or grave injury to the health, whether physical or mental of the pregnant woman, whether before, at, or after the birth; or
       (2) When there is substantial risk that if the child were born it would suffer from such physical or mental abnormalities as to be seriously handicapped in life.
    b. Abortion should be carried out only at the place where the woman normally resides.
    c. It shall be compulsory for the doctor to give information about each case of abortion to the prescribed authority.
    d. Doctors having conscientious objection to inducing abortion may have the right to refuse to do so.
    e. That only trained gynaecologists should be allowed to perform the operation.
    f. That if a woman having at least three children wants an abortion, the sterilization operation may also be performed on her with her consent.

16. West Bengal	The Government of West Bengal supports the recommendations of the Committee on the liberalization of abortion.
17. Nagaland	The State Government has indicated that according to a special provision of Article 371 a of the Constitution of India, no Act of Parliament will be applicable to Nagaland unless specifically recommended by the Nagaland Legislative Assembly. Consequently State Government cannot offer any comments in the matter at present.

Union Territory

1. Andaman and Nicobar Islands	The recommendations of the Committee are acceptable to the Administration

2. Chandigarh — The Union Territory is of the considered opinion that the abortion law be amended, and that it should be liberalized. This will not only help family planning, which should be adopted as a national religion, but will also curb and do away with illegal abortionists, who are doing more harm than good in the community. Many a time women are brought to the hospitals after an attempted abortion by quacks in a very precarious condition and may even die without any proper medical aid of excessive haemorrhage or sepsis. In many advanced countries, even in countries with a less serious population problem than ours, abortion has been legalized, in an attempt to lessen the dangers of illegal abortions. The Chandigarh Administration is of the view that if legalized termination of pregnancy could be done under ideal surgical conditions for family planning and health reasons, etc., it becomes most desirable that it should be liberalized.

3. Dadra and Nagar Haveli — The Administration agrees with the recommendations of the Committee and also the supplementary notes thereon and endorses the suggestion of amending the existing provisions of IPC. The term 'police officer' should also be defined as suggested by Dr Shivapuri.

4. Delhi — The Executive Council is against the liberalization of abortion as it may lead to several social evils. It agrees however that permission for termination of pregnancy by a qualified medical practitioner may be extended to the following categories after it has been certified by a Board of at least three medical persons, duly nominated for this purpose by the State Government:

(i) Where there is a substantial risk that if the child was born it would suffer from such physical or mental abnormalities as to be seriously handicapped in life on account of a family history of insanity, mental deficiency or any disease relating to one or both of the parents.

(ii) Where the pregnancy has resulted from rape and *prima facie* evidence to that effect is available to the Board. The fact that a report alleging rape was lodged with the police or a complaint was filed before a

	magistrate may be deemed to be sufficient evidence for this purpose.
5. Goa, Daman and Diu	The Administration agrees with the Shantilal Shah Committee Report and observation made by Dr Shivapuri in paragraph 4 of his supplementary note regarding definition of police officer.
6. Himachal Pradesh	The Administration is in general agreement with the views put forward by the Committee formed by the Government of India on the liberalization of abortion laws.
7. Laccadive, Minicoy and Amindivi Islands	The Administration agrees with recommendations of the Committee.
8. Manipur	(i) Recommendations made in paragraphs 4.2 (i) (a), (b) and (c) on pages 61 and 62 of the report pertain to medical conditions. This will not help the family planning programme by reducing the birth rate substantially.
	(ii) If the object of the report is to legalize abortion for purposes of reducing the birth rate in respect of the family planning programme, abortions should be legally permitted in all cases of married persons who do not want to have a child for any reason whatsoever—medical, social, economic, etc. Unless this is done, the liberalization of the law on purely medical grounds as stated above will not give a licence for legalized abortion to the medical practitioner.
	(iii) *Vide* paragraph 2.63, it has been summarized in paragraph 35 that generally it is the married women who resort to induced abortion. The surmise is based on almost all studies conducted in foreign countries.
	(iv) The qualifications of the medical practitioner who has been allowed to terminate the pregnancy, *vide* the recommendation in paragraph 4.2 (i) on page 61, have not been prescribed. Generally speaking, medical practice is permitted to all registered medical practitioners in the country. The registration laws of medical practitioners differ from State to State. In certain States even unqualified persons with some experience of medical practice

	have been registered by the States as 'medical practitioners'.
	(v) Due to underdeveloped facilities for operations for abortions in medical institutions and also because of inadequately/not trained staff, the risk in performing the operations will be considerable.
	(vi) The problem of family planning should be tackled by social scientists, medical sociologists, social workers, etc., instead of ordinary medical graduates/clinically-oriented medical officers.
9. North East Frontier Agency (N.E.F.A.)	As the family planning programme has been taken up on a very limited scale, the question of considering legalized abortion does not arise at present.
10. Pondicherry	4.2 (i) (a). Definition of the term 'serious risk to life' should be specified. 4.2 (i) (b). No comments. 4.2 (i) (c). Unmarried women from puberty to menopause (including mentally defective women and widows). 4.2 (ii) (a)–(d). No comments. 4.3. No comments. 4.4. No comments. 4.5. (a)–(d). No comments. 4.6. No comments.
11. Tripura	The Administration has no comments to offer.

THE JOINT SELECT COMMITTEE'S REPORT

The Joint Select Committee of the Parliament at their first sitting on 30 January 1970 decided to invite memoranda on the Bill from various associations, organizations and individuals interested in the subject matter of the Bill. The Committee also decided to invite witnesses to give oral evidence on the Bill.

The Committee held nineteen sittings between 30 January 1970 and 3 November 1970 when witnesses representing medical and legal professions, women's associations and certain religious groups gave oral evidence. The Committee received memoranda and suggestions on the Bill from twenty-one persons and associations. Twenty-six witnesses tendered evidence before the Committee. The Committee finalized their Draft Report on the Bill by the end of 1970 and presented it to the Parliament.

The major changes suggested by the Committee in the Bill and the reasons for such changes are:

Clause 1

New Clause 6 inserted in the Bill provides for framing of rules by the Central Government to carry out the provisions of the Act generally and, in particular, to prescribe experience or training which a registered medical practitioner should have if he intends to terminate any pregnancy under the Act. Further, Clause 7 (original Clause 6) empowers the State Governments to make regulations on certain matters provided in the Act. As it might take some time before these rules and regulations are framed and finalized by the Governments concerned, the Committee feel that practical difficulties would arise if the Act came into operation immediately. The Committee, therefore, feel that the Act should come into operation after the rules and regulations have been framed by the Governments concerned. A new sub-clause has, therefore, been inserted empowering the Central Government to appoint, by notification in the Official Gazette, a date on which the Act will come into force.

Clause 2

Paragraph (a). Under sub-clause (4) of Clause 3, the consent of the guardian has been made obligatory for the termination of pregnancy of a woman when the latter is either a minor or a lunatic. In the circumstances, the expression 'guardian' has been so defined by the Committee as to cover not only the guardian of a minor but also the guardian of a lunatic.

Further, the Committee are of the opinion that, for the purposes of this Act, it would be sufficient if the person having the care of the person of the minor or lunatic is defined as the guardian. The Committee have, therefore, omitted reference to the person having the care of the property of the minor, so that a person having the care of the property only of the minor or lunatic may not exercise the powers conferred on the guardian by the Act.

Paragraph (d). As the termination of pregnancy is a delicate operation and, at times, involves serious complications and even danger to the life of the pregnant woman, the Committee are of the opinion that such an operation should be carried out only by those registered medical practitioners who have the requisite experience or training in gynaecology and obstetrics and that the experience or training which a registered medical practitioner must possess in this regard, should be prescribed by rules made by the Central Government. Accordingly, the Committee have amended the definition of the expression 'registered medical practitioner'.

Clause 3

The Committee are of the opinion that for the termination of a pregnancy, where the length of pregnancy exceeds 12 weeks but does not exceed 20 weeks, it is not necessary that two registered medical practitioners should act together. It would suffice if, in such a case, the opinion of two registered medical practitioners, formed in good faith, is in favour of termination of the pregnancy and the actual operation is carried out by a single registered medical practitioner. The Committee have amended sub-clause (2) of the clause to clarify the position.

Original sub-clause (4) made separate provisions for consent to be obtained for terminating pregnancies of a married woman when such pregnancy is alleged to have been caused by rape, or of a widow who is a minor or lunatic or of an unmarried girl who had not attained the age of 18 years or of an unmarried woman who, being above the age of 18 years, was a lunatic. The Committee feel that except in the case of termination of pregnancy of a woman who has not attained the age of 18 years or who is a lunatic, obtaining of such a consent should not be made obligatory. The Committee have, therefore, substituted the revised paragraph (a) for the original paragraphs (a), (b), (c) and (d) of the sub-clause.

The other changes made in the clause are of a verbal or clarifying nature.

Clause 5

The Committee are of the opinion that the relaxation provided in this clause in the matter of length of pregnancy should extend only to cases where termination of the pregnancy is necessary to save the life of the pregnant woman and that it should not extend to cases where it is necessary to terminate a pregnancy to save permanent grave injury to the physical or mental health of the pregnant woman. Necessary changes have, therefore, been made in the clause.

In view of the amendment in paragraph (d) of Clause 2, registered medical practitioner referred to in this clause would mean a registered medical practioner who has experience or training in gynaecology and obstetrics. The Committee feel that where the termination of a pregnancy is immediately necessary to save the life of the pregnant woman, the provision with regard to experience or training in gynaecology and obstetrics should not be insisted upon so that such pregnancy may be terminated, where necessary, by a general practitioner. An explanation to that effect has been added to the clause.

Clause 6 (New)

This new clause is consequential to the amendment carried out in paragraph (d) of Clause 2.

The other changes made in the Bill are of a consequential or drafting nature.

The Committee recommend that the Bill, as amended, be passed.[3]

The Bill, as recommended by the Joint Select Committee, with the noted few minor changes, was passed by the Rajya Sabha (Upper House) on 27 May 1971 and by the Lok Sabha (Lower House) of the Indian Parliament on 7 August 1971.

The Bill as passed follows:

THE MEDICAL TERMINATION OF PREGNANCY ACT, 1971
NO. 34 OF 1971

(10 August 1971)

An Act to provide for the termination of certain pregnancies by registered medical practitioners and for matters connected therewith or incidental thereto.

Be it enacted by Parliament in the Twenty-second Year of the Republic of India as follows:

1. (i) This Act may be called the Medical Termination of Pregnancy Act, 1971.
   (ii) It extends to the whole of India except the State of Jammu and Kashmir.
   (iii) It shall come into force on such date as the Central Government may, by notification in the Official Gazette, appoint.
2. In this Act, unless the context otherwise requires,
   (a) 'Guardian' means a person having the care of the person of a minor or a lunatic;
   (b) 'Lunatic' has the meaning assigned to it in section 3 of the Indian Lunacy Act, 1912;
   (c) 'Minor' means a person who, under the provisions of the Indian Majority Act, 1875, is to be deemed not to have attained his majority;
   (d) 'Registered medical practitioner' means a medical practitioner who possesses any recognized medical qualification as defined in clause (h) of section 2 of the Indian Medical Council Act, 1956, whose name has been entered in a State Medical Register and who has such experience or training in gynaecology and obstetrics as may be prescribed by rules made under this Act.
3. (i) Notwithstanding anything contained in the Indian Penal Code, a registered medical practitioner shall not be guilty of any offence under that Code or under any other law for the time being in force, if any pregnancy is terminated by him in accordance with the provisions of this Act.

---

[3] Parliament of India: *The Medical Termination of Pregnancy Bill, Report of the Joint Committee* (New Delhi, Rajya Sabha Secretariat, November, 1970), pp. 4 and 5.

(ii) Subject to the provisions of sub-section (iv), a pregnancy may be terminated by a registered medical practitioner,
  (a) where the length of the pregnancy does not exceed twelve weeks, if such medical practitioner is, or
  (b) where the length of the pregnancy exceeds twelve weeks but does not exceed twenty weeks, if not less than two registered medical practitioners are,
of opinion, formed in good faith, that:
  (i) The continuance of the pregnancy would involve a risk to the life of the pregnant woman or of grave injury to her physical or mental health; or
  (ii) There is a substantial risk that if the child were born, it would suffer from such physical or mental abnormalities as to be seriously handicapped.
  Explanation 1: Where any pregnancy is alleged by the pregnant woman to have been caused by rape, the anguish caused by such pregnancy shall be presumed to constitute a grave injury to the mental health of the pregnant woman.
  Explanation 2: Where any pregnancy occurs as a result of failure of any device or method used by any married woman or her husband for the purpose of limiting the number of children, the anguish caused, by such unwanted pregnancy may be presumed to constitute a grave injury to the mental health of the pregnant woman.
(iii) In determining whether the continuance of a pregnancy would involve such risk of injury to the health as is mentioned in sub-section (ii), account may be taken of the pregnant woman's actual or reasonably foreseeable environment.
(iv) (a) No pregnancy of a woman, who has not attained the age of eighteen years, or, who, having attained the age of eighteen years, is a lunatic, shall be terminated except with the consent in writing of her guardian.
  (b) Save as otherwise provided in clause (a), no pregnancy shall be terminated except with the consent of the pregnant woman.
4. No termination of pregnancy will be made in accordance with this Act at any place other than:
  (a) A hospital established or maintained by Government, or
  (b) A place for the time being approved for this Act by Government.
5. (i) The provisions of section 4, and so much of the provisions of sub-section (ii) of section 3 as relate to the length of the pregnancy and the opinion of not less than two registered medical practitioners, shall not apply to the termination of a pregnancy by a registered medical practitioner in a case where he is of opinion, formed in good faith, that the termination of such pregnancy is immediately necessary to save the life of the pregnant women.
  (ii) Not withstanding anything contained in the Indian Penal Code, the termination of a pregnancy by a person who is not a registered medical practitioner shall be an offence punishable

under that Code, and that Code shall, to the extent, stand modified.

Explanation. For the purpose of this section, so much of the provisions of clause (d) of section 2 as relate to the possession, by a registered medical practitioner, of experience or training in gynaecology and obstetrics, shall not apply.

6. (i) The Central Government may, by notification in the Official Gazette, make rules to carry out the provisions of this Act.
   (ii) In particular, and without prejudice to the generality of the foregoing power, such rules may provide for all or any of the following matters, namely:
   (a) The experience or training, or both, which a registered medical practitioner shall have if he intends to terminate any pregnancy under this Act; and
   (b) Such other matters as are required to be, or may be, provided by rules made under this Act.
   (iii) Every rule made by the Central Government under this Act shall be laid, as soon as may be after it is made, before each House of Parliament while it is in session for a total period of thirty days which may be comprised in one session or in two successive sessions, and if, before the expiry of the session in which it is so laid or the session immediately following, both Houses agree in making any modification in the rule or both Houses agree that the rule should not be made, the rule shall thereafter have effect only in such modified form or be of no effect, as the case may be; so, however, that any such modification or annulment shall be without prejudice to the validity of anything previously done under that rule.
7. (i) The State Government may, by regulations:
   (a) Require any such opinion as is referred to in sub-section (ii) of section 3 to be certified by a registered medical practitioner or practitioners concerned, in such form and at such time as may be specified in such regulations, and the preservation or disposal of such certificates;
   (b) Require any registered medical practitioner, who terminates a pregnancy, to give intimation of such termination and such other information relating to the termination as may be specified in such regulations;
   (c) Prohibit the disclosure, except to such persons and for such purposes as may be specified in such regulations, of intimations given or information furnished in pursuance of such regulations.
   (ii) The intimation given and the information furnished in pursuance of regulations made by virtue of clause (b) of sub-section (i) shall be given or furnished, as the case may be, to the Chief Medical Officer of the State.
   (iii) Any person who wilfully contravenes or wilfully fails to comply with the requirements of any regulation made under sub-section

(i) shall be liable to be punished with a fine which may extend to one thousand rupees.
8. No suit or other legal proceeding shall lie against any registered medical practitioner for any damage caused or likely to be caused by anything which is in good faith done or intended to be done under this Act.

Thus the proposal to re-examine the restrictive, century-old law on abortion, made in August 1964, ended in August 1971 with the enactment of a liberal and progressive measure, the Medical Termination of Pregnancy Act of 1971. Within the short period of seven years India was able to pass in a commendable, democratic fashion a far-reaching measure assuring the women of India freedom from undesirable and unwanted pregnancies. This new law is a major landmark in India's social legislation.

It will be noticed that the Indian law on abortion, the Medical Termination of Pregnancy Act, 1971, which came into force on 1 April 1972, while generally modelled after legislation of its kind, particularly the British enactment, does however make a significant departure.

The Act permits the termination of pregnancy by a registered medical practitioner where the length of the pregnancy does not exceed twelve weeks, or by two registered medical practitioners, acting together, where the length of the pregnancy exceeds twelve weeks but does not exceed twenty weeks, provided that the medical practitioner or practitioners are of the opinion that (1) the continuance of the pregnancy would involve a risk to the life of the pregnant woman or an injury to her physical or mental health; or (2) there is a substantial risk that if the child were born it would suffer from such physical or mental abnormalities as to be seriously handicapped.

The explanatory notes provide two cases where continued pregnancy is assumed to constitute a grave injury to the mental health of the pregnant woman, namely (1) where a pregnancy is alleged by a pregnant woman to have been caused by rape; and (2) where the pregnancy occurs as a result of failure of any device used by a married woman or her husband for the purpose of limiting the number of children.

This provision constitutes a healthy innovation and provides a physician of conventional and perhaps unimaginative bent of mind a broad interpretation of the basic concept of the potential injury to the mental health of the pregnant woman.[4]

Further, in deciding whether the continuance of a pregnancy would

---

[4] The present writer wanted to make the Indian law simple and grant abortion virtually on demand because an overwhelming majority of Indian women are married at a relatively early age, and by and large seek abortion only after the

involve a risk to the physical or mental health of the pregnant woman, the Indian law permits some consideration of the pregnant woman's actual or reasonably forseeable environment. This socio-medical provision taken from the British Abortion Act of 1967, coupled with the earlier provision, makes the Indian law quite liberal and in keeping with the health and demographic needs of the nation.

Now that abortion has been legalized it remains to be seen what happens to a major argument advanced against the liberalization of abortion in India: that the existing medical facilities in terms of qualified physicians and surgeons (particularly gynaecologists) and hospital beds are inadequate even for the normal needs of the present population, and a permissive abortion law would put an intolerable strain on the existing medical services.

It is difficult to meet this argument, for there is no way of accurately projecting the magnitude of the possible demand for abortion. It will take some time, at least a year or two, before the liberal provisions of the new Act become known to women in all the remote rural areas of the country. It is also not known how cooperative and helpful the members of the medical professions, both in and outside the government services, will be in interpreting the Act and meeting the needs of the pregnant women in question. The government's formal stand is that it is a health measure and will not normally be used for birth control, but everyone concerned with India's welfare hopes it will. An educated guess would indicate a million women as the approximate number who would make use of the law in the first year. The number of women demanding abortion services would no doubt increase in the coming years but it is difficult to predict their exact number. It would depend on such factors as the tempo at which sterilization is carried out, the general availability of contraceptive services, and the national educational campaign informing the adult citizen of both the magnitude of the nation's population problem and the various measures made available to solve it.

Soon the average Indian mother must be made to realize firstly that it is better for all concerned and much easier to use a contraceptive than to become pregnant; secondly, that it is a lot simpler to

---

arrival of the fifth or sixth baby, from a back street abortionist; and after trying unsuccessfully a variety of indigenous means of controlling conception. But the writer failed to obtained a consensus on this point from his ministerial colleagues.

In India the wife's desire for a small family is based on both economic and health grounds. Poverty, low income or a low level of living could have been made grounds for abortion but these proved vague and imprecise concepts in a country where the majority are 'poor'. Hence this innovation, so that few women would be denied abortion which, in the Indian context would be a necessary supplement to, though not a substitute for, contraception.

have an abortion in the first trimester of pregnancy for health or economic reasons than to deliver a baby and take care of it; and lastly, that if the woman should want a family, she should stop at two. Surely, delivering 20 million babies annually would be a greater strain on the nation's medical services and economic resources than, say, performing one to five million abortions a year.

This Act, if imaginatively interpreted and executed, can meet such problems as adverse sex ratio and raising large families in the hope of obtaining a son. It could also mean the prolongation of the mother's life, and, of course, small families with better living conditions.

If the sex of the embryo or foetus could be predicted, some mothers would want to abort a female foetus if they already had daughters, apart from the fact the family might be materially poor and the parents unable to meet certain minimum requirements of infant and child care. A third or fourth daughter in a poor, orthodox and un-emancipated family longing for a son will mean poor nutrition and veiled psychological rejection for the child. If malnutrition continues into adolescence and later, the damage to the next generation can be serious.

Such abortions could really be therapeutic, for the future mothers of the country deserve special care, as their physical stamina, mental health and psychological attitudes are of basic importance. What is really needed is a fundamental change of attitudes toward girls in the culture of many communities in India. This is easier said than done. At least the physical and in the long run genetic damage can be prevented by selective abortion.

Under the above circumstances a male foetus in certain orthodox communities need not be aborted unless, of course, it is defective. If a healthy baby boy is born and receives poor nutrition his future role as a father may be less adversely affected than would that of a future mother, not to speak of the health of the generations yet unborn. This appears discriminatory but may protect the health and welfare of the next generation.

Lastly, the fact that India has legalized abortion does not necessarily mean that it is always available to every pregnant woman who would like to terminate her early pregnancy. The reason for this is that the majority of the population, being in rural areas and far away from government hospitals and clinics, have no access to the facilities promised by the government. And equally important is the fact that it will take some time before the information that abortion is now legal and available reaches all the needy mothers in India. Another problem is the existing adverse doctor/population ratio, as well as the doctor/pregnant mother ratio. This has to be improved as a part of the overall improvement in the total health infra-structure by increasing the number of general physicians, gynaecologists, and obstetricians, in particular, and the overall para-medical personnel.

DEMOGRAPHIC EFFECTS OF ABORTION

The experience of family planning clinics in India during the last decade has been that a majority of abortions were demanded because of contraceptive failure. The demand was considered illegal under the law of that time, though the pregnant women were unaware of the law, and consequently their requests for abortions were denied.

Married women who visit family planning clinics for contraceptive services for either limiting or spacing births often find that they have failed to prevent a pregnancy despite their use of contraception. The major reasons for such failures have almost always been either an imperfection in the contraceptive used or inability to use it correctly. While precise figures are lacking, the percentage of contraceptive failure in India has been much higher than is usually supposed. Such women usually think in terms of terminating their pregnancies. Having motivated the couples, particularly the wives, to consider the small family a desirable objective, there appears to be no point in telling them, 'You can only go so far in attaining this ideal and no further'. Motivated women consider induced abortion merely an extension of the logic of contraception.

And yet few countries have come out in favour of induced abortion specifically as a method of population control. The communist countries, as pointed out earlier, contend that the legalization of abortion is to guarantee women's freedom and acknowledge their right to decide how many children they are willing to bear and rear.

Almost all countries stress safeguarding the pregnant woman's health as a major factor in permitting abortion and some also include such factors as poverty and a blighted social environment. Still others have maintained that liberalized abortion laws would curb illegal abortions and their undesirable consequences, since women, for a variety of reasons, resort to abortion, no matter what the law says. Even Japan, faced with the loss of her empire and the repatriation of her colonists and soldiers, and overall bleak economic prospects at the end of the Second World War, in passing her Eugenic Protection Law granting permissive abortion in 1948, never explicitly admitted that overpopulation was the reason for such legislation.

No matter what the particular circumstances in any country for liberalizing abortion laws, there is no doubt that these permissive laws and the incidence of induced abortion affect the nation's birth rate. Needless to add, there are such other relevant factors as the number of women in the reproductive age group, the age at marriage, the knowledge, extent and effectiveness of contraception used by the couples, and overall religious and social *mores*.

The impact of liberal abortion laws and the resulting high incidence of induced abortion on a nation's fertility level can be examined if detailed data on all the relevant factors are available for a continuous and fairly long period of time. For such a study the Soviet Union, Sweden, the socialist European countries (Bulgaria, Hungary, Poland, the German Democratic Republic, Czechoslovakia, Romania) and Japan provide good examples.[5] But complete statistics for all the liberal years since abortion has been permitted in all these countries are not available. However, Japan and Hungary, which may be taken as fairly representative on this subject, have the necessary statistics and can be examined for an evaluation of the demographic effects of abortion.

JAPAN

Among the Asian countries Japan was the first to liberalize its abortion law, in a rather roundabout way. With the termination of the Second World War, Japan, as already observed, not only lost her colonies but had to repatriate 3·1 million soldiers and other military personnel, and 3·2 million colonists and civilian administrators, and find a place for a total population of about 80 million in a war-devastated homeland.

Japan's birth rate before the beginning of the Second World War in 1939 was 26·6 per 1,000 of the population but it rose to 34·3 in 1947 with the return of millions of young men from overseas and the consequent baby boom. The death rate before the war was 15·7 and this declined to 14·6 in 1947, and afterwards even more rapidly. In fact, population pressure on the home islands was one of the major reasons that drove Japan to war, but the war, far from solving the population pressure, made it worse.

It is not clear whether in 1948 the government passed the Eugenic Protection Law to meet the nation's demographic pressure. The objective of this measure was 'to prevent the increase of the inferior descendants from the standpoint of eugenic protection and to protect the life and health of the mother as well'. Under this law several family planning methods including induced abortion were made available. As for abortion, 'it was stipulated that a legal induced abortion must be performed in conformity with the regulations pre-

---

[5] The abortion law was liberalized in Bulgaria and Poland in April 1956, in Hungary in June 1956, in Romania in September 1956, in Czechoslovakia in December 1957 and in Yugoslavia in February 1960.

scribed in the law and by a "designated physician" who had been authorized by the local medical association.'[6]

The next year the Act was amended to include financial considerations, apart from purely medical grounds, as a reason for permitting induced abortions. This led the way for a national programme of subsidized abortion.

Japan was able to carry out successfully this policy of induced abortion. Japan's literacy rate, even among females, was high even before the war, in fact higher than the rate in the United States of America. For an Asian nation, Japanese women occupied an advanced position and were liberated in many ways. On the subject of abortion and contraception, Japan fortunately did not have to labour under traditional cultural or religious inhibitions which more conventional Asian cultures and the Christian West had to cope with. When adverse economic and social circumstances compelled a drastic cut in the country's birth rate, Japan rose to its task.

By 1953 the nation could claim, despite the ravages of the war, 692 public and 55 private clinics. Some 20,000 pharmacies put up door plates announcing the availability of a 'contraceptive consultant'. The newspapers with circulations running into millions and other mass media carried on enlightened propaganda in favour of population control. As a result, the number of abortions increased from 320,000 in 1950 to 1,280,000 in 1958, or from 137 to 682 per 1,000 live births. The result was a dramatic and definitive decline in the birth rate from 34·3 per 1,000 in 1947 to 17·2 in 1957—exactly halved in a decade. A remarkable achievement indeed.

The question now is: how much did induced abortion contribute to this decline in the nation's birth rate? The following table makes instructive reading.

Table 5. Numbers and Rates of Pregnancies, Abortions and Births in Japan, 1947–1957

Year	Pregnancies	Abortions	Births	Pregnancies	Abortions	Births
	(in thousands)			(per 1,000 of population)		
1947	Not known	Not known	2,700	Not known	Not known	34
1949	2,800	100	2,700	34	1	33
1951	2,600	500	2,100	30	5	25
1953	2,900	1,100	1,800	33	12	22
1955	2,900	1,200	1,700	32	13	19
1957	2,700	1,100	1,600	29	12	17

[6] M. Muramatsu, 'Action Programmes in Family Planning in Japan', in M. Muramatsu and P. A. Harper (eds), *Population Dynamics* (Baltimore, the Johns Hopkins Press, 1965), p. 70.

It is probable that in any given year more than one abortion may have been required to prevent a single birth. According to Heer,[7] two or even three abortions may be required in the absence of contraception to avoid one birth because the interval between two conceptions will be longer when the first one results in a live birth than when it is terminated by abortion. Potter,[8] however, fixes the interconception interval at about nine months when the first pregnancy is terminated by abortion—three months of pregnancy, one month of post-partum amenorrhea, and five months of ovulatory exposure before the second conception.

Muramatsu estimates the impact of abortion on Japan's fertility by calculating (1) the potential reproduction without contraception or abortion, and (2) the effectiveness of contraception. The difference between the contraceptive effectiveness figure and the hypothetical pure birth rate yields an estimated birth rate influenced by abortion.[9] In fact, the abortion figures in the table are less than the actual ones, for as Muramatsu points out, 'In summary, it can be stated that the number of live births in 1955 in Japan would have amounted to twice (or more) the number actually registered, if there had been no induced abortion at all. And the reporting of induced abortions to the health authorities probably included only 50 to 60 per cent of all cases actually performed'.[10]

It is a remarkable fact that during the last half of the decade during which Japan halved her birth rate, well over a million Japanese women resorted to abortion every year. That is, roughly out of every five women who became pregnant, at least two got the pregnancy terminated.[11] But if the official figures represent certain underregistration, then annually about 2 million pregnant women resorted to abortion.

---

[7] D. M. Heer, 'Abortion, Contraception and Population Policy in the Soviet Union', *Demography* (1965:2).
[8] R. G. Potter, Jr, 'Birth Intervals: Structure and Change', *Population Studies* (November 1963).
[9] Minoru Muramatsu, 'Effect of Induced Abortion on the Reduction of Births in Japan', *Milbank Memorial Fund Quarterly* (April 1962).
[10] ibid.
[11] The present writer on his numerous visits to Japan since the Second World War to study her population problems *vis-à-vis* induced abortion was surprised to discover the large number of abortions middle-class Japanese women had undergone in quest of a small family. Women questioned at random in various cities and villages in the decade after the war gave the pat answer that they did not mind two or three abortions within a couple of years. It is debatable why such a disciplined and enterprising people as the Japanese did not take to contraception instead of abortion. And had they taken to contraception as wholeheartedly as they took to abortion, it is to be wondered whether the birth rate would have declined as rapidly and definitively as it did.

Since 1955 there has been a gradual decline in the annual number of abortions; and efforts, official and private, have been made to switch the birth control-minded population from the wasteful and expensive method of induced abortion to contraception. And now the Japanese authorities are complaining of a labour shortage and hoping that the present birth rate of 19 per thousand (1971) will increase.

Thus while there is no doubt that the rapid decline in Japan's birth rate was achieved by abortion, the incidence being much higher than the official figure, there is, however, some misconception that abortions *alone* were responsible for the decline in fertility. While the Japanese people did not resort to contraceptives during the decade under review, there were quite a few sterilizations, both vasectomies and tubectomies, as revealed by the following table:

Table 6. Sterilizations in Japan, 1949–1956*

Year	Total	Year	Total
1949	5,356	1953	31,162
1950	10,792	1954	36,601
1951	15,409	1955	41,273
1952	21,241	1956	42,662

* As quoted in Thomas O. Wilkinson, 'Japan's Population Problems', in S. Chandrasekhar (ed.), *Asia's Population Problems* (London, Allen & Unwin; New York, Praeger, 1967), p. 115.

Thus both abortions and sterilizations contributed to the remarkable decline in Japan's birth rate.

HUNGARY

Of all the east European socialist countries which, in the wake of the Soviet Union, legalized abortion, with certain variations to meet particular national needs, the experience of Hungary comes closest to that of Japan. After the Second World War Hungary, faced with a loss of manpower like most European countries, embarked on a pro-natalist policy. These measures led to a rise in the nation's birth rate to 23·0 per 1,000 by 1954.

But in 1956 the Hungarian government reversed its pro-natalist policy and liberalized its abortion law. The available data reveal that within a decade Hungary achieved the lowest fertility rate in the world, a birth rate of 12·9 per 1,000 in 1962. Apart from the communist ideology, the desire for a better level of living, the increasing number of women entering the labour force, particularly the professions as in the Soviet Union, and the growing exodus of people from rural agricultural areas to relatively industrialized urban areas have been some of the factors responsible for the decline in the birth rate. In a word, a desire for higher socio-economic standards in terms of levels of consumption has been the dominant factor behind these abortions.[12]

To begin with, abortion, as in almost all countries, was not unknown in Hungary before the war, though it is difficult to estimate the pre-war incidence of illegal abortions. For a short period, 1949–52, abortions were permitted for medical indications only. In 1953 personal, socio-economic and eugenic indications were added to therapeutic grounds resulting in a striking increase in the number of legal abortions. In 1956 a new and simplified abortion law came into force, authorizing a woman 'to make a conscious determination of desired family size and... to interrupt an undesired pregnancy by means of an induced abortion'. This meant virtually abortion on demand, for the pregnant woman's wish was considered more important than any particular health, economic or social indication. The result was a steep rise in legal abortions, to about 20 per 1,000 population in 1968.[13]

In Hungary, as in most European socialist countries, abortion is free for medical indications and only a nominal fee is charged for other cases. Almost all the abortions are done in public hospitals and the patient's stay under normal conditions does not exceed two days. The women receive the best available care.

It is, however, somewhat surprising for a European country that in Hungary the knowledge of modern contraception is not widespread, particularly in the rural areas. Nearly 40 per cent of the women interviewed in a survey expressed ignorance of modern contraception, and they had not come across any birth control literature; nor did they receive any information on the subject from the mass media. But they all knew about abortion. There is apparently some communication gap as far as a large segment of women are concerned because condoms and other conventional contraceptives are available at cheap rates in many shops. Only in 1967 did Hungary begin to

[12] E. Szabady, *Some Problems of Fertility and Population Development* (Budapest, Hungarian Academy of Sciences, 1966).
[13] During a visit to Hungary in 1969 the Minister of Health of the Hungarian People's Republic arranged for me to address a large women's audience in Budapest under the joint auspices of the Ministry of Public Health and the Hungarian Academy of Science, of which the Demographic Research Institute is a part. Dr E. Szabady, the Director of the Demographic Research Institute, was in charge of the meeting. After my lecture dealing with the Indian population problem and India's plans to liberalize abortion, I asked the audience what was their idea of the maximum number of children a couple should have. The unanimous response was, 'One or two are more than enough'.

manufacture an oral contraceptive, 'Infecundin'. And in 1968 a Hungarian physician, Dr K. Hotey, brought out a new contraceptive 'film' for local use by men and women. It appears, however, that fewer than 5 per cent of Hungarian couples use modern contraceptives.

Thus Hungary for the period under review seems to have relied largely on abortion, and apparently no official effort was made to spread contraceptive information. Dr E. Szabady, the distinguished Hungarian demographer, believes that if effective contraception had been made available, a quarter of the induced abortions during the period could have been prevented. The picture is now being changed, and Hungarian women in the future may resort to abortion only in cases of contraceptive failure and certain other special circumstances.

Table 7. Numbers and Rates of Pregnancies, Abortions and Births in Hungary, 1956–1966.*

Year	Pregnancies	Abortions	Births	Pregnancies	Abortions	Births
	(In thousands)			(per 1,000 population)		
1956	316·4	123·6	192·8	32·0	12·5	19·5
1957	330·1	162·9	167·2	33·6	16·6	17·0
1958	341·4	183·0	158·4	34·5	18·5	16·0
1959	340·9	189·7	151·2	34·3	19·1	15·2
1960	342·5	196·0	146·5	34·4	19·7	14·7
1961	344·1	203·7	140·4	34·3	20·3	14·0
1962	327·7	197·6	130·1	32·5	19·6	12·9
1963	340·2	207·9	132·3	33·7	20·6	13·1
1964	350·8	218·7	132·1	34·5	21·5	13·0
1965	347·0	214·0	133·0	34·2	21·1	13·1
1966	359·0	220·5	138·5	35·3	21·7	13·6

* The figures for abortions and live births are official. The total number of pregnancies may be a little higher to provide for still births, figures for which are not available.

CONCLUSION

What lessons can India draw from the abortion experience of Asia and Europe and particularly from that of Japan and Hungary? India's concern is to protect the health of women from both excessive births and quack abortionists. To begin with, what is likely to happen to India's current estimated annual 5 million illegal abortions? The liberalization of abortion laws does not necessarily or always lead to a decline in the number of illegal abortions, much less their complete disappearance. The reason is that legal and illegal abortions may attract different kinds of patients. In any community there will always be a small number of unmarried, widowed, divorced or separated women, who, when they become pregnant, prefer secret abortion to a legal one in a public hospital. On the other hand, it is also possible that once abortion laws are liberalized the hidden illegal abortions surface and are replaced by legal abortions.

Therefore it is possible that if the availability of legal abortion is known to all the pregnant women of India and if hospital facilities are made available for all in need of abortions for various valid reasons, it may be assumed that there could be a demand for some 5 million abortions a year in the country. This number would include some of the old illegal abortions as well as some women who are seeking abortions in the light of the new legal provisions and who otherwise might not have sought an illegal abortion.

What is likely to be the impact of the new abortion law on India's birth rate? Any attempt to answer this question must involve knowledge of *how* the nation's general (public) hospitals under state governments will interpret the Act. If the demographic pressure is even overtly admitted as a reason for abortion, then pregnant mothers with three living children should be eligible for abortions. This, apart from abortions for genuine health reasons, can mean a tremendous load on the existing not too adequate or efficient health and medical services in the country. The situation can, of course, be remedied by improving the present hospital services and by developing the nation's health infra-structure which is now virtually non-existent.

Today fewer than 20 per cent of India's total of roughly 105 million couples practise any kind of family planning method. What will be the effect of permissive abortion on the non-contracepting behaviour of India's population? First, those couples in the reproductive age groups who have undergone either vasectomy or tubectomy can be eliminated from the total. As for those dependent on the loop or condom or any other method (only relatively few are on the pill), will the availability of abortion induce them to relax or continue the careful use of the available contraceptives? Will fashions suddenly change and abortion become socially acceptable and popular, as, for instance, vasectomy is today? It is difficult to answer these questions in the absence of any empirical data.

However, if the experience of Japan and Hungary has any relevance for India, which has between 1 and 5 million abortions per year (the estimate for illegal abortions is 5 million out of more than 20 million pregnancies per year), with the present tempo of sterilizations of between 500,000 and a million per year, and the current rate of conventional contraceptive uses, she should be able almost to halve her birth rate within a decade. This is nothing more than an educated guess in the absence of detailed 1971 census data on age, sex, marriage and family size. The next ten years, 1972–82, should provide the needed statistics on abortion and allied matters, and these together with the 1981 census figures should be able to tell us how effective abortion, along with other family planning methods, will be in reducing India's birth rate from her present 38 to about 20 per 1,000.

In conclusion, the role of abortion in our society, whether it is for demographic, eugenic, economic, legal, medical or humanitarian purposes, must encompass in the near future the following credo:

1. The fundamental right to choose whether to bear children or not is a right of privacy which no law of any country, no matter what its religious affiliation or political ideology, should curtail.

2. Abortion must be made available on demand while gynaecologists, psychiatrists and social workers might be permitted to counsel the pregnant woman to the contrary. But the pregnant woman's decision must be final, subject only to the safety of her person.

3. Abortion in the last analysis must be a matter left entirely to the pregnant woman and her physician. (Of course, there are millions of sick and suffering women in the world who have no physician to consult at all.)

4. No distinction should be made between married and unmarried women, unless the pregnant woman is less than sixteen years of age, when the consent of parents or guardian should be obtained.

5. A woman must be able to obtain an abortion, if necessary, free of charge in an approved, tax-supported clinic or hospital. But if any fee is to be charged in such an institution it must be based on the principle of ability to pay, without impairing in any way the quality of service.

6. The woman must be thoroughly informed of all the available and effective methods of family planning so that she can avoid the need for further abortions.

7. The hospital and other relevant authorities must keep the identity of the woman undergoing abortion confidential for it is the woman's private concern.

Appendix 1

THE LEGAL STATUS OF ABORTION IN SELECTED COU[NTRIES] 1971[1]

Category[2]	Countries
1. Laws authorizing abortion on *demand*	Hungary, USA (Alaska, Hawaii and New York states), USSR
2. Laws authorizing abortion on *ethical and humanitarian* grounds (e.g. rape, incest, sexual relations with a minor or a person with mental disease or deficiency)	Colombia, Jordan, Lebanon. Countries which permit abortion on social and socio-medical grounds also come in this category
3. Laws authorizing abortion on *social* grounds	Bulgaria, Czechoslovakia, Denmark, East Germany, Finland, India, Poland, Romania, Singapore, Tunisia and Yugoslavia
4. Laws authorizing abortion on *socio-medical* grounds	Denmark, Finland, Iceland, India, Japan, Norway, Sweden, United Kingdom and USA (Oregon)
5. Laws authorizing abortion on *medical* grounds	Argentina, Brazil, Canada, Cameroun, Ethiopia, Honduras, Israel, Morocco, Peru, Switzerland, Syria, Turkey, Thailand and USA (California, Colorado, Georgia, Kansas, Maryland and N. Carolina)
6. Laws authorizing abortion only to *save the life* of the pregnant woman	Albania, Austria, Cambodia, Chile, France, Iran, Italy, Mexico, Pakistan, Peru, Senegal, Syria, USA (certain states), Venezuela and Western Australia
7. Laws prohibiting abortion under any circumstances, even when the life of the pregnant woman is in danger	Dominican Republic, Ireland, the Philippines, Portugal and Spain

[1] *Abortion Laws: A Survey of Current World Legislation* (Geneva, World Health Organization, 1971), *passim*.
[2] This table gives only broad generalizations. These are conditioned by certain administrative and bureaucratic controls (e.g. the agreement of two physicians or the consent of a medical board), time limit (usually the first trimester of pregnancy), certain medical and other contra-indications such as purulent foci and a previous abortion within the preceeding six months etc.

Appendix 2

LIST OF DISEASES WHICH ARE MEDICAL INDICATIONS FOR ARTIFICIAL INTERRUPTION OF PREGNANCY

1 Internal Diseases

(a) *Diseases of the heart and of the vascular system:*
Valvular defects, in particular mitral stenosis and aortic insufficiency with reduced heart performance or valvular defects which, before pregnancy, have given rise to signs of circulatory difficulty or infarction of the lungs or embolisms in the systemic circulation or an acute pulmonary oedema.
Acute or progressive inflammatory diseases of the heart (myocarditis, bacterial endocarditis, progressive rheumatism).
Infraction of the myocardium.
All heart diseases causing up to the end of the third month of pregnancy arythmias (auricular flutter, auricular fibrillation, heart syncopes), venous statis or cyanosis. Congenital heart defects with circulatory disorders, especially defects accompanied by cyanosis or coarctation of the aorta with noticeable pressure on the upper extremities.
Hypertension.
Marked varicose veins, in particular in the region of the reproductive organs and the lower extremities with antecedent ulcers and thrombophlebitis.

Note: In the case of a slight cardiopathia, consideration must be given to whether the mother can be sufficiently protected from all effort (household duties, employment, care of the infant especially during the first two to three years, several young children in the family who need supervision even at night).

(b) *Pulmonary diseases:*
Pulmonary diseases with reduced respiratory function (pulmonary insufficiency), bronchietasis, chronic bronchitis, emphysema.
Chronic pulmonary infections.

(c) *Renal diseases:*
Chronic glomerulonephritis, with symptoms of an active inflammatory process, increased blood sedimentation.
Chronic glomerulonephritis accompanied by nephrotic or hypertonic syndrome.
Chronic pyelonephritis.
Nephrosis accompanied by hyperproteinaemia.
Amyloidosis of the kidneys.

(d) *Blood formation diseases:*
Haemorrhagic diseases.
All haemoblastoses and all haematoplastomias.

Affections of the bone marrow.
Haemolytic anaemia.

(e) *Diseases of the digestive organs:*
Complicated cholelithiasis (biliary cirrhosis, choledocholithiasis, biliary empyema, cholangitis, pancreatitis).
Relapsing pancreatitis, pancreatolithiasis.
Ulcer.
Colitis ulcerosa.
States of denutrition caused by diseases of the digestive organs.
Chronic parenchymatic diseases of the liver.
State after infectious hepatitis within a period of two years or when there are signs of functional liver troubles.

(f) *Disorders of the endocrine glands:*
Exophthalmatic goitre.
Goitre with mechanical sequelae, in particular retrosternal goitre with compression of the cervical vessels.
Hypothyreoses.
Hypophysial adenoma with mechanical sequelae, especially with threat to the vision.
Hyperparathyreoses.
Diabetes mellitus: when there is a hereditary taint on both sides (diabetes mellitus of both parents or in both families); with a tendency towards acidosis; that reacts poorly to insulin treatment; diabetes, accompanied by certain complications, in particular vascular complications occurring in young people and having repeatedly caused miscarriages or still births.
Addison's disease: after preparation in a specialized establishment for the purpose of preventing an Addisonian crisis.
Adenoma of the suprarenals.
Other endocrinopathias detected on examination in a specialized establishment.

(g) Infectious diseases in the first three months of pregnancy which are transmissible to the foetus and cause malformation or maldevelopment of the foetus.

2. Surgical Diseases

Large abdominal hernias, diaphragmatic and hiatus hernia if the woman concerned does not consent to an operation.
Syndromes following stomach or gall bladder resection.
Relapsing ileus.
Congenital anomalies of the large intestine and of the rectum which have been treated surgically.
Extensive abdominal and pelvic tumours.
State after surgical intervention on the internal secretion organs.
State after lung resection with reduced pulmonary functional capacity.

Pulmonary actinomycosis and pulmonary abscesses.
Advanced organic changes in the peripheric vessels.
Genuine or false arterio-venous aneurysms of the aorta and of the large vessels of the abdomen and the extremities.
Benign anatomic malformations of the cerebral vessels.

3. Urological Diseases

State after removal of a kidney or if a kidney is missing (agenesia) or stunted (hypoplasia).
Cystic degeneration of the kidneys with bilateral renal deficiency.
Haematuria of unknown origin.
Bilateral nephrolithiasis, even if the concretions are not fixed and are often spontaneously eliminated from both kidneys—uratic urolithiasis.
Unilateral nephrolithiasis with reduction of renal function.
Papillomatosis of the bladder.
Hydronephrosis.
Dystopic kidney, crossed dystopia, and horseshoe kidney.

4. Orthopaedic Diseases

Pelvic malformation as a result of an accident. Chrobak pelvis, central dislocation of the hip joint.
Symphysiolysis due to delivery.
Scoliosis of the lumbar and thoracic regions of the vertebral column with malformation of the pelvis.
Malformation of the pelvis with osteomalacia and Paget's disease.
Spondylolisthesis.
Subluxation and other malformations of the hip joint, possibly state after Perthe's disease (account must be taken of whether the mother can suitably care for the child when she has difficulty in moving).
Bilateral ankylosis of the hips.
Arthritis deformans of the hips and lumbosacral arthritis.
State resulting from extensive and complicated fractures of the long bones and from intra-articular fractures of the large joints.
Diseases of the skeletal system (such as osteopsathyrosis, Albers-Schönberg disease) even where only the father is suffering therefrom, chondrodystrophia foetalis.
Osteomalacia.
Paralysis of the abdominal muscles after poliomyelitis, especially when the lower extremities are also paralysed.
Relapsing chronic osteomyelitis of the pelvic bones.
Spastic paralysis (Little's disease).

5. Rheumatic Diseases

Spondylarthritis ankylopoietica (Bechterew's disease) when the hip joints are attacked at the same time.

APPENDIXES

Chronic progressive polyarthritis when the hip joints are especially attacked.
Chronic polyarthritis complicated by amyloidosis.

6. Oncological Diseases

All malign tumours regardless of their site, and states following their surgical removal or irradiation treatment.

7. Tuberculosis

(a) *Pulmonary tuberculosis:*
  (aa) All contagious and potentially contagious forms of tuberculosis.

  (ab) All forms of tuberculosis (even where Koch's bacillus has not been isolated) at the progressive stage (decomposition, dissemination, infiltration) or at the resorption stage or with active symptoms (sub-composition, decomposition).

  Note: Especially when complex treatment is unlikely to avert the risk of aggravation of tuberculosis in the mother and when it is not possible to prevent the child from becoming infected.

  (ac) All non-contagious and inactive forms which may again become active or be aggravated as a result of pregnancy, delivery, or breast feeding, in particular in young mothers where a preceding pregnancy was a factor in the occurrence or aggravation of tuberculosis; when the disease has been inactive for only a short time; when little time has elapsed since the last pregnancy; in a multipara, when the cardio-respiratory function is diminished; in the case of tuberculosis complicated by a serious non-specific disease which, at the stage at which it manifests itself, would not in itself have constituted a sufficient indication for interruption of pregnancy (diabetes mellitus).

(b) *Extra-pulmonary tuberculosis:*
Tuberculosis of the larynx.
Tuberculosis of the vertebral column, of the pelvic bones, of the hips, of the knee joints, and of the other bones.
Intestinal tuberculosis.
Urogenital tuberculosis.
Tuberculosis of the nervous system and tubercular meningitis.

Note: All forms of tuberculosis in young persons require particularly careful assessment. Contagious tuberculosis in the father is also an indication for interruption of pregnancy if he cannot be isolated because of housing conditions; interruption of pregnancy is also indicated if a tubercular mother is forced to give up her work, thereby endangering the orderly routine of her life.

8. Diseases of the Nervous System

Disseminated cerebrospinal sclerosis and other demyelination diseases.
Paraplegia and serious paraparesis of the lower limbs, of organic origin.

Tumours of the brain, of the spinal cord, and of their envelopes.
Parasitogenic diseases of the central nervous system.
Hereditary ataxia (Friederich's disease) and cerebral heredo-ataxia (Marie's disease).
Hepato-lenticular degeneration (Wilson-Westphal-Strümpell's disease).
Myopathias.
Dystrophic myotonia.
Huntington's disease.

Note: Huntington's disease and distrophic myotonia is an absolute indication for artificial interruption of pregnancy even if only the father suffers therefrom.

Cerebral form of endarteritis obliterans.
Encephalo-malacia regardless of the cause.
Aneurisms and intra-cranial vascular malformations.
Funicular myelosis.
Epidemic encephalitis in the acute or chronic stage.
Other encephalites in the acute stage.
Prolonged acute stages of other neuro-infections.
Myasthenia.
Syringomeyelia and syringobulbia.
Haematomyelia.
Intra-cranial and spinal arachnitis with objective neurological findings.
Meningorrhagia.
Traumata of the brain and of the spinal cord with clear focal symptomatology (including residual states of this type).
Serious post-meningitis residual states.
Double athetosis.
Primary atrophia of the cerebellum.
Progressive lordotic dysbasia.
Periodic family paralysis.
Serious lymbardiscopathia.
Neuralgia of the trifacial nerve.
Epilepsy accompanied by general degeneration and character changes, when other somatic and psychic deficiencies are present; when the patient is recalcitrant to undergo a modern drug therapy; when the spouse suffers at the same time from severe headache.
Status epilepticus.

9. Psychiatric Disorders

(a) *Diseases of the mother:*
Delirious states becoming worse during pregnancy.
Progressive paralysis.
Chronic schizophrenia.
Generation psychosis with repeated attacks.
Serious manic melancholia.
Serious psychopathia.
Serious reactive psychic disorders with possible suicidal tendencies.

Serious obsessional and anxiety neurosis.
Heredo-family nervous diseases with psychic disorders.

(b) Diseases of one of the spouses, especially one which may be communicated to heredity.
Oligophrenia.
Serious psychopathias.

(c) When the mother has already had by the same father an oligophrenic or otherwise stigmatized psychopathic child.

(d) Serious chronic alcoholism of one of the spouses showing itself in character disorders.

10. Dermato-venereal Diseases

(a) *Venereal diseases:*
Syphilis: Malign sero-positive in the second stage; manifest in women who cannot tolerate specific therapy including antibiotics; malign in the third stage especially when organic; choroiditis, atrophy of the optic nerve, and syphilitic changes in the auditive nerve: sero-resistant accompanied by fear of passing on syphilis to the child (relative indication after consultation with a psychiatrist).
Neurosyphilis and tabes dorsalis.
Syphilitic spondylitis.
Extensive cicatricial and ulcerous changes in the region of the genital organs and of the perineum in the case of Nicolas-Favre's disease.

(b) *Skin diseases:*
Pemphigus vulgaris, p. foliaceus, p. vegetans and Senear-Usher syndrome.
Erythrodermia.
Pruriginous diseases persisting over several years accompanied by psychopathic disorders.
Diffused scleroderma.
Acute dermatomyositis.
Mycosis fungoides.
Necrobiosis lipoidica diabeticorum.
Purpura becoming worse during pregnancy.
Impetigo herpetiformis.
Advanced ichthyosis.
Hereditary palmar and plantar keratosis.
Hrythematodes acutus, possibly acute disseminatus.
Hereditary bulbus epidermolysis.
Xeroderma pigmentosum.
Bourneville-Pringle's disease (epiloia).
Dermatitis herpetiformis Duhring.
States following serious burns accompanied by cicatricial and cheloidal changes on the bosom and around the genital organs.

11. *Eye Diseases*

(a) Toxic inflammations of the optic nerve.

(b) Certain diseases of the organ of sight, when a permanent lesion of the eye may be averted by means of interruption of pregnancy; mechanical lesions of the optic nerve, inflammation of the retina and of the choroid membrane, haemorrhage in the corpus vitreum, serious lesion of the cornea, acute glaucoma.

(c) Pronounced myopia with displacement of the retina or vascular lesion, with haemorrhages of the retina or when degenerative changes at the back of the eye occur.

(d) Congenital total cataract in the mother or in one of her children accompanied by other congenital phenomena.

(e) Hereditary and family degeneration of the retina and the optic nerve.

12. *Ear, Nose, and Throat Diseases*

(a) Otosclerosis accompanied by serious psychosis (opinion of a psychiatrist together with an ear specialist); when serious reduction of hearing has occurred as a result of a preceding pregnancy; otosclerosis in both the father and the mother.

(b) Hereditary deafness or serious hereditary impairment of hearing.

13. *Gynaecological and Obstetrical Diseases*

(a) Hyperemesis gravidarum, ptyalism.

(b) Late gestosis, especially when associated with hypertension or albuminuria and regardless of the stage of pregnancy.

(c) Pathological states in the obstetrical anamnesis.
Repeated atonic haemorrhages after delivery.
Repeated haemorrhages associated with adherence of the placenta which would have to be removed by hand.
After two deliveries which have required Caesarian operations.
When there is habitual uterine inertia.
After adjustment by operation of a support or suspension apparatus, if the woman has two living children.
When there is venter pendulus caused by diastasis of the rectus after two deliveries.
Late gestosis especially when pregnancy follows shortly on delivery.

(d) Chorea gavidarum.

(e) Foetal anomaly, repeated births of children suffering from foetal erythroblastomatosis if there have been two prior still births or the foetuses have been damaged.

(f) Conception occurring after temporary sterilization by X-rays or if the ovaries have been damaged during irradiation by X-rays administered for other purposes.

(g) Conception before the age of 16 if pregnancy has been discovered by the third month.

(h) Conception after the age of 45 years.

Appendix 3

QUESTIONNAIRE OF THE COMMITTEE TO STUDY THE
QUESTION OF THE LEGALIZATION OF ABORTION

No. 4–6/55–FPII
Dated 24th February, 1965

From
    Shri Shantilal H. Shah
    Minister for Health, Law and Judiciary, Maharashtra and Chairman of
    Committee to Study the Question of Legalization of Abortion

Dear Friend:

In pursuance to the recommendation of the Central Family Planning Board, the Ministry of Health, Government of India, has set up a Committee to study the question of legalization of abortion in the country. This Committee can succeed in its task only with your co-operation. I have no doubt, your support will be readily forthcoming.

I am forwarding a questionnaire for your views on the subject of abortion which will be of assistance to the Committee in formulating their recommendation. The collection of reliable data is difficult. The name of the person giving information will be treated confidential, if so desired. No punitive action against any individual will be taken by the Committee based on the information supplied. I will be grateful if you could send the required information. I am conscious that the time available is very short but I will be grateful if the required information is sent by the 31st March, 1965, to me c/o Director, Family Planning, Directorate General of Health Services, Patiala House, New Delhi.

                                                Yours sincerely,
                                                Shantilal H. Shah

Questionnaire on Abortion

NOTE: I   For the purpose of this questionnaire the term 'abortion' or interruption of pregnancy will mean the discharge of the foetus and its appendages from the mother at a period when the foetus is unable to keep its life outside the mother's body, i.e. before it has become viable, which period is about twenty-eight weeks of pregnancy.

           II   Section 312 of the Indian Penal Code runs as follows:

                        312, Whoever voluntarily causes a woman with child to miscarry shall, if such miscarriage be not caused in good faith for the purpose of saving the life of the woman, be punished with imprisonment of either description for a term which may extend to three years, or with fine, or with both; and, if the woman is quick with child, shall be be punished with imprisonment of either description for a term which may extend to seven years, and shall also be liable to fine.

Explanation: A woman who causes herself to miscarry is within the meaning of this section. The word miscarriage used in the section includes not only abortions but also expulsion of viable foetus before the normal birth. The only exception is in case of a miscarriage caused in good faith for the purpose of saving the life of the mother.

III Wherever possible please indicate the basis on which you have given the reply, the source of information and/or your reasons.

PART I

1.1 What is in your view the estimated yearly number of
- A. Spontaneous abortions
- B. Induced abortions
    - (1) Legal, that is, to save the mother's life
    - (2) Illegal
        - a. For birth control
        - b. For other reasons

(Please specify the area and the period covered by the answers.)

1.2 What are in your view the reasons for which people resort to
- A. Illegal abortion for
    - (1) Birth control
    - (2) Other reasons

To what extent do these reasons operate in both cases?

1.3 Is the incidence of illegal abortions increasing? If so the extent of the increase during the last ten years and the reasons therefor.

1.4 Do you think married persons (a) who are not able successfully to practise birth control, and (b) others who do not practise birth control resort to illegal abortion?

1.5 What are the methods known to you for inducing illegal abortions?

1.6 Are there local illegal abortionists in
- A. Urban areas
- B. Rural areas

1.7 What are the fees of local illegal abortionists in
- A. Urban areas
- B. Rural areas

1.8 What age group of women resorts to illegal abortions and for what reasons?

1.9 Are they performed
   A. For economic reasons, or
   B. For unwanted pregnancies posing a serious threat to the health of the mother?

PART II

2.1 Would you favour legalization of abortions for those women in whom pregnancy occurred and to whom birth of an additional child would cause serious threat to health of the mother? In such cases, should there be a provision for conducting abortion by a qualified medical person?

2.2 If you consider that abortions for socio-economic reasons should not be legalized, state your reasons.

2.3 Would you support legalization of abortion for social and economic reasons? If so
   A. Under what conditions, and
   B. At what state of pregnancy should the operation be resorted to?

2.4 Do you consider that the abortion should be permitted in the following cases:
   A. If due to the mother's illness, physical defect or weakness, childbirth would result in serious danger to her life or physical or mental health.
   B. If the pregnancy is a result of rape, criminal coercion or incestuous sexual intercourse.
   C. If the mother is insane or imbecile.
   D. (1) If either spouse has a hereditary disease or defect transmissible directly to the offspring (List I).
      (2) If both the spouses are carriers of a detectable hereditary trait which causes a serious or a fatal disease when it is in double dose in the offspring (List II).
      (3) If the couple has already produced a child with a hereditary disease or defect that has a high degree of recurrence in families (List III).
      (4) If the spouses are blood relations and one of their near relatives has produced an offspring with a hereditary disease or defect of the type given in List III. For Lists I, II and III mentioned above, see paragraph 4.1.
   E. If either spouse is suffering from leprosy which is liable to be contagious to the child.
   F. If either spouse is suffering from tuberculosis which is liable to be contagious to the child.
   G. If the mother has already three children and is willing to get sterilized concurrently with abortion.

APPENDIXES

   H. If the mother has already three children but is not willing to get herself concurrently sterilized nor her husband.

   I. If the mother has three children and both husband and wife are willing to get sterilized.

2.5 In cases G, H and I, would you prefer a birth at full period with sterilization immediately thereafter?

2.6 In case you consider inclusion of any or all the above conditions under which abortions should be permitted, are you in favour of the following safeguards? (Please state 'yes' or 'no'.)

   A. Opinion of three medical men, i.e.

   (1) The attending physician,

   (2) Gynaecologist, and

   (3) A specialist qualified to give opinion on defects for which abortion is desired.

   B. A board including a lawyer, a gynaecologist and a responsible citizen (not related to the patient) to consider the proposal for abortion.

   C. What other safeguards, if any, would you suggest?

2.7 Do you consider that in every case the application for abortion should be made

   A. By the woman herself, or

   B. By her guardian if the woman is under age or placed under guardianship if imbecile or is unable to give legal consent due to mental derangement?

2.8 Are you in favour of abortion being permitted in case of unmarried woman or widow generally?

2.9 Do you think that penalties should be imposed for performing permissible abortion by persons not medically qualified to do so?

2.10 In what cases would you consider making sterilization compulsory after an induced abortion?

PART III

3.1 Do you consider that artificial abortion is a sin against society, religion and culture?

   A. In all cases.

   B. Except for reasons mentioned in Question 2.4 and, if so, which of them? Please state your reasons.

PART IV

(Answers to Part IV are requested from members of the medical profession only.)

4.1 Do you consider that the following diseases and disorders may be considered for the purposes of paragraph 2.4 (D) above? Please state 'yes' or 'no' against each.

List I. Dominant and sex-linked diseases and defects.
1. Achondroplasia
2. Aniridia
3. Christmas disease
4. Diabetes insipidus
5. Epidermolysis Bullosa
6. Epiloia
7. Haemophilia
8. Huntington's chorea
9. Manic-depressive psychosis
10. Marfan's syndrome
11. Microphthalmos
12. Muscular dystrophy
13. Neurofibromatosis
14. Osteogenesis imperfecta
15. Partial albinism with deafness
16. Polychthaemia vera
17. Polyposis of colon
18. Retinoblastoma
19. Spherocytosis (achluric Jaundice)
20. Total hereditary deafness

List II. Diseases which could be prevented by laboratory tests on parents.
1. Sickle-cell disease
2. Thalassemia major and other thalassemia diseases
3. Erythroblastosis foetalis

List III. Recessive diseases and defects.
1. Albinism
2. Alkaptonuria
3. Amyotonia congenita
4. Anophthalmos
5. Diabetes mellitus
6. Fibrocystic disease of pancreas
7. Galactosuria
8. Gargoylism
9. Hereditary ataxia
10. Ichthyosis congenita

11. Infantile amaurotis idiocy
12. Laurence-Moon-Biedl syndrome
13. Methemoglobineamia
14. Myoclonic epilepsy
15. Optic atrophy (Leber's disease)
16. Phenvlketonuria
17. Retinitis pigmentosa
18. Schizophrenia
19. True microcephaly
20. Wilson's disease

(You may suggest any other disease or disorder which in your opinion should be considered.)

PART V

Kindly intimate any other information or observations which you consider will be useful to the Committee to assess the extent of the problem, its effect on individual and society and any action that may be taken. Such information or observation may be sent in the form of a brief memorandum not exceeding 2,000 words. It may also be stated if the views expressed are personal or of an organization or a group.

Note: If the views expressed are of an organization or group, the name and address of the organization or group and the number of members in the organization or group may be stated. In all cases give name, profession and address (including name of place, district and State) in block letters.

Appendix 4

AN ANONYMOUS REPORT OF ILLEGAL ABORTIONS DONE IN AN INDIAN CLINIC

This confidential report has been prepared by reputable investigators who cannot be identified for obvious reasons. The report is based on personal investigations and highlights a vital maternal health problem. Copies are forwarded to the Ministry of Health and Family Planning for such use as may be deemed fit.

Summary

Data are presented from an illegal abortion centre in an Indian metropolitan area. An analysis has been made on 404 persons, of whom 32 per cent had diagnosis confirmed by gross or microscopic examination of the curettings.

Eighty-seven per cent of these persons report themselves as married although internal evidence suggests that perhaps only 72 per cent were married. Most are within the age group 20–29, the average age being 27·6 years which approximates the average age of persons who accept loops and pills in India. The average number of pregnancies per person is 4·3; the average number of living children (2·5) is significantly lower in those who accept loops and pills.

The patients reported that 24 per cent of their pregnancies previous to this study were aborted and 42 per cent of their total pregnancies (including those of this study) were aborted; both figures are well above the accepted spontaneous abortion rate of 10 per cent.

No morbidity or mortality data are available.

Introduction

There are no Indian studies of the type of person who seeks illegally induced abortions and very little factual data is available other than the second-hand information deductible from septic or incomplete abortions that may come into hospitals. Therefore it seemed wise to gather minimal data on the characteristics of the women who seek out such services, and who might be regarded as a sample of what is occurring in metropolitan areas for illegally induced abortions.

Materials and Methods

The data included in this report have been voluntarily collected from an apparently well-organized and fairly large abortion team in an Indian metropolitan area. The director of the group is a graduate of a leading medical college in India and has a Diploma in Obstetrics and Gynaecology from that same institution.

There are two clinics at which the services are provided; one is in the centre of the city, quite near the medical college, and the other is a nursing home located in one of the outlying parts of the city. The city clinic provides abortion services to women within the first trimester of pregnancy; more advanced cases are cared for at the nursing home. Patients are referred by satisfied customers or by doctors who do not perform abortions; a collector system has been established including private transport to fetch and deliver patients. For those cases in whom serious problems occur during the office surgery, the vehicle of the organization can deposit the unidentified patient at the casualty department of the nearby medical college hospital. The director did not disclose any data relating to the incidence of complications or mortality. He did describe periodic payments for protection to the local police.

Patients enter the clinic waiting room; when their turn comes they are taken into a minimally equipped operation theatre, and following the completion of the abortion they are led into one of two small rooms with beds where they rest for thirty minutes or more before leaving with their families or being delivered by the organization's car. Attached to the theatre is a combined scrub and clean-up room in which the operator washes his hands with soap and water and in which an ayah scrubs the instruments in soap and water before placing them to soak.

There are three sets of instruments which are in constant rotation in the cycle of (1) in use, (2) being scrubbed, (3) being soaked in Dettol solution. The duration of the soaking varies according to the number of patients to be attended to that day. On the occasion of one observation visit, ten abortions were performed as D and C's within one hour; and at the time of leaving the office twenty patients were counted in the waiting room. Thus the time for sterilization is inadequate, although inspection of the scrubbed instruments confirmed that they were thoroughly cleansed.

The D and C is performed as follows: the patient, in her own clothes, is put on an operating table which is provided with stirrups. She is then given 25 mg of pethidine intravenously from a syringe and needle which is used for all patients that day; the needle is wiped with alcohol between patients. Her feet are put into the stirrups and a pelvic assessment is made by the operator with freshly washed hands. A tray of instruments in Dettol is conveniently placed; the operator washes the vulva with cotton swabs soaked in Dettol. A Sims retractor brings the cervix into view and the anterior lip is caught with a tenaculum. The cervix is rapidly dilated with a series of Hegar dilators until the *os* will admit a sponge forceps. The operator then makes an attempt with the sponge forceps to remove the conceptus as nearly intact as possible, following which he very rapidly evacuates the remaining products with in-and-out movements of the sponge forceps, grasping with each motion another fragment and bringing it into the vagina. The vagina is cleaned out at convenient intervals. The uterine cavity is wiped out with a cotton pledget of Dettol held in the sponge forceps. On some cases he uses a sharp curette and demonstrates to the observer the familiar grating sound of curetting the myometrium. When the uterus seems empty and the bleeding minimal (massage was used once, and intravenous ergot was available on the side table), a Dettol-soaked cotton tampon is placed in the vagina and the patient is assisted to the adjacent recovery room.

The staff for the operating theatre consisted of a former compounder who is the expert abortionist; the physician, who holds the Diploma in Gynaecology and Obstetrics, is occasionally in the theatre or available by telephone, but seldom does the routine jobs himself. There were two female assistants in the room, one administered the intravenous pethidine and the other stood at the patient's head to explain and comfort. The ayah who scrubbed the instruments was not directly involved but was fully occupied in the rotation of instruments.

All patients are routinely given broad spectrum antibiotics to be taken orally for the next few days. The director was clearly pleased with the efficiency of the organization and seemed to be concerned that the standard of care and technique should be as good as possible. However, when the disadvantage of repeated use of the same IV needle was pointed out, it did not seem likely that any change was in the offing. He was keenly interested at the suggestion that an iodine sterilization procedure might be more effective in the limited time available than Dettol.

The suburban nursing home was found to have a much better equipped operating theatre. Facilities for autoclaving instruments and drapes, for general anaesthesia, and for nursing care seemed more adequate. The procedure usually employed there was to introduce a sterile rectal tube into the uterus and to leave it in place for twenty-four hours to induce labour. At the time of the observation visit there was one case in the six-bed institution that had been treated in this manner the week before; and at the time of the introduction of the catheter, massive bleeding was provoked. An unsuspected placenta praevia was pre-existing in this twenty-week pregnancy. The director was miles away on the other side of the city when this accident occurred; by telephone he was able to contact a qualified surgeon (FRCS) who lived only two blocks away and who came to the rescue for the necessary hysterotomy. Anaesthesia, sterile instruments and drapes, and assisting staff were inadequate for this procedure. The patient had survived the procedure without benefit of transfusion and apparently was recovering well.

For this study small cards printed with seven queries were furnished to the city clinic and completed for 404 patients. The following information was received: marital status, urban or rural residence, age and education of the patient, number of total pregnancies, number of previous abortions, number of living children. A total of 423 patients were reported over a three-month period from this clinic; of these the information on 19 patients was considered inadequate or internally inconsistent, therefore only 404 cases have been analysed. After 105 patients were reported in the first month, it was thought wise to ask for the surgical specimens from each reported patient to confirm the diagnosis in each procedure.

In the third month 188 patients were reported and of these 143 consecutive cases had surgical specimens collected in formalin and forwarded to us. Of these 11 were broken, and one case presented twins; thus 132 patients had specimens for examination, which provided possible confirmation of diagnosis in 32 per cent of the total number of cases. Forty-seven appeared to the naked eye to be genuine abortion specimens owing to the obvious presence of an embryo or foetal parts; the remaining 84 were analysed microscopically.

Table 4 (a). Pathological examination of 132 specimens (30% of reported cases)

	Per cent of total	No. of patients
Positive evidence of pregnancy	—	95
Gross[1] (foetal parts)	47	
Microscopic	78	
	125	
Negative or doubtful evidence of pregnancy		5
Negative	1	
Decidual reaction only	6	
	7	

[1] Visible without microscopic examination.

Thus there was only a 5 per cent error in the diagnosis of first trimester pregnancy from this clinic.

The average case-load was only 5 cases per working day, according to the reports received, with a range of cases per day of 1 to 34. The director of the service acknowledged that all cases were not included, as some women, frightened or suspicious when the information was requested, refused to co-operate and could not be included. A second important deterrent to complete coverage was that the individual assigned to fill out the cards was also the individual who drove the transport, and therefore he was not always available to keep the records.

Although no accurate register is kept, the Director estimates that they abort a total of 450 patients a month, an average of 15 patients per day. In the first two weeks of the month there are 30 or more patients daily and on holidays and festivals there is also a large number; towards the end of the month the daily case-load decreases to 4 or 5. During the five-month-period of this study, an estimated 2,250 patients were seen at the clinic from which 20 per cent provided the information that has been analysed.

The information provided for this study has been validated through observation visits to the clinic, the internal consistency of the data, and through confirmation of the diagnosis of pregnancy by examination of the specimens received. Although the data on the specimens may have been tampered with, there is no reason to doubt the general truth of the material as it was freely offered for inspection after reasonable assurance that the confidence of the source would not be betrayed.

Results

Approximately 87 per cent of the patients who were reported in this study are married. The distribution by marital status and urban or rural residence is presented in Tables 4 (*b*) 1 and 4 (*b*) 2. In this distribution there appears to be a larger proportion of married women from a rural residence amongst those from whom specimens were obtained than in the total group of patients.

Table 4 (b). Distribution of 404 patients seeking abortion according to their marital status and residence

4 (*b*) 1. *All patients*

	Married	Unmarried	Total
No.	351	53	404
Per cent	86·9	13·1	100

	Urban	Rural	Urban	Rural	
No.	217	134	42	11	404
Per cent	53·7	33·2	10·4	2·7	100

4 (*b*) 2. *Patients from whom specimens were obtained*

	Married	Unmarried	Total
No.	116	15	131
Per cent	88·6	11·4	100

	Urban	Rural	Urban	Rural	
No.	63	53	12	3	131
Per cent	48·1	40·5	9·2	2·2	100

In Table 4 (*c*) the average of selected characteristics of patients with specimens is compared with the averages of all patients. The values are almost the same in both groups but the patients with specimens are seen to have a significantly higher average number of pregnancies and a higher average number of previous abortions. This may be accounted for by a larger proportion of patients from rural residence in the group that had confirmed diagnoses.

The lower averages of the total number of patients may be taken as minimal average characteristics.

Table 4 (c). Selected average characteristics according to availability of surgical specimens of 404 patients having an illegally induced abortion in an Indian metropolitan area

Per cent of total number	All patients 100 (actual no. 404)	Patients with specimens 32·5 (actual no. 131)
Age in years	27·5	27·4
Education in years	6·8	5·7
Total pregnancies	4·3	4·8
Total living children	2·5	2·5
Number of previous abortions	0·8	1·2

APPENDIXES

Table 4 (d) presents the distribution of patients according to selected characteristics. This shows that almost 60 per cent of the patients were between 20 and 29 years of age. Approximately 60 per cent have more than 6 years of schooling, which includes 20 per cent with matric or higher levels. The patients with specimens have a slightly lower level of education.

Thirty-five per cent of all patients have had 1–3 pregnancies; 40 per cent have had 4–6 pregnancies; patients with specimens have had slightly more.

Approximately 20 per cent of patients have no living children and 75 per cent have fewer than four living children.

The outstanding characteristic is that 50 per cent of all patients have had a previous abortion; the fact that 86 per cent of patients with specimens have had previous abortions may be because of the special selection made in the choice of these patients, which included more rural women.

There is no information as to whether the 'previous abortions' were spontaneous or induced.

Table 4 (d). Distribution of 404 patients having an illegally induced abortion by selected characteristics and according to the availability of surgical specimens

		All patients (404) Per cent	Patients with specimens (131) Per cent
Age in years	0–19	8·1	9·9
	20–29	58·9	58·0
	30–39	28·5	29·0
	40+	4·5	3·1
		100·0	100·0
Education in years	0	17·8	26·0
	1–5	20·3	22·1
	6–10	42·1	37·4
	Matric +	19·8	14·5
		100·0	100·0
Total no. of pregnancies	1–3	41·3	32·1
	4–6	40·4	46·6
	7+	18·3	21·3
		100·0	100·0
Total no. of living children	0	20·8	17·6
	1–3	53·7	53·4
	4–6	20·0	25·2
	7+	5·5	3·8
		100·0	100·0
No. of previous abortions	0	49·3	13·7
	1	32·9	61·8
	2–5	17·8	24·5
		100·0	100·0

In Table 4 (*e*) the average value of selected characteristics has been exhibited according to the marital status. In summary, it shows that the married patients (87 per cent of all) are older, with less education, but have more pregnancies, more living children, and more previous abortions.

Table 4 (e). Selected average characteristics according to marital status of 404 patients having an illegally induced abortion

	Married patients	Unmarried patients
Per cent	86·9 (actual no. 351)	13·1 (actual no. 53)
Age in years	28·5	21·4
Education in years	6·3	9·6
Total pregnancies	4·7	1·5
Total living children	2·8	0·6
No. of previous abortions	0·8	0·4

The distribution of married and unmarried patients is set down in Table 4 (*f*) and clearly confirms the average values of Table 4 (*e*).

Unmarried patients are younger (43 per cent less than 20 years old), better educated (38 per cent are matric level or above); have fewer pregnancies (96 per cent have no more than 3), have fewer living children (only 2 per cent have living children) and have had less experience with previous abortions (70 per cent have had none).

Table 4 (f). Distribution of 404 patients having an illegally induced abortion by selected characteristics and according to marital status

		Married (actual no. 351) Per cent	Unmarried (actual no. 53) Per cent	Total (actual no. 404) Per cent
Age in years	0–19	4·0	43·4	8·1
	20–29	60·1	50·9	58·9
	30–39	31·9	5·7	28·5
	40+	4·0	—	4·5
		100·0	100·0	100·0
Education in years	0	19·7	5·7	17·8
	1–5	22·5	5·7	20·3
	6–10	40·7	50·9	42·1
	Matric+	17·1	37·7	19·8
		100·0	100·0	100·0

Table 4 (*f*)—cont.

		Married (actual no. 351) Per cent	Unmarried (actual no. 53) Per cent	Total (actual no. 404) Per cent
Total no. of pregnancies	1–3	33·0	96·2	41·3
	4–6	45·9	3·8	40·4
	7+	21·1	—	18·3
		100·0	100·0	100·0
Total no. of living children	0	9·1	98·1	20·8
	1–3	61·6	1·9	53·7
	4–6	23·1	—	20·0
	7+	6·2	—	5·5
		100·0	100·0	100·0
No. of previous abortions	0	46·2	69·8	49·3
	1	34·8	20·8	32·9
	2–5	19·0	9·4	17·8
		100·0	100·0	100·0

Tables 4 (*g*) and 4 (*h*) relate experience with abortion according to parity level and according to the number of living children. The levels of abortion identified are in excess of the standard 10 per cent level of spontaneous abortion for those patients with fewer than 7 pregnancies, indicating that persons who go in for abortion as a method of birth control tend to do so repeatedly.

Table 4 (g). Percentage of patients having one or more previous abortions according to the total number of pregnancies

No. of pregnancies	No. of patients	Per cent having one or more previous abortions
1	57	0·0
2	43	32·6
3	67	49·3
4	70	51·4
5	58	74·1
6	33	75·8
7	25	68·0
8	30	66·6
9	11	90·0
10	6	100·0
11	3	33·4
12	1	0·0

Twenty-eight per cent of the patients seeking abortion in this study have no living children; as only 13 per cent of those with no living children admit to being unmarried, this point may be interpreted as internal evidence that a significantly larger percentage (15 per cent) were actually unmarried even though they claimed to be married.

Table 4 (h). Percentage of patients having one or more previous abortions according to the total number of living children

No. of living children	No. of patients	Per cent having one or more previous abortions
0	83	27·7
1	63	54·0
2	82	59·8
3	73	52·1
4	41	70·7
5	22	63·6
6	18	58·6
7	16	37·5
8	3	66·6
9	2	0·0
10	1	0·0

Comment

Table 4 (i) gives comparative values of patients accepting loops, pills or sterilization in the Indian Family Planning Programme.

Table 4 (i). Comparative characteristics of family planning acceptors according to contraceptive methods
(between this anonymous abortion study and two other official studies)

Method	Age (median years)	Living children	Education with more than 4 years of school (per cent)	Continuation rate at 12 months (per cent)
IUCD[1]				
Urban	29·5	4	50	69–78
Rural		?	?	57–73
Pill[2]				
Urban	27·6	3·5[3]	62	65
Rural	29·2	3·5[3]	22	
Sterilization[1]				
Vasectomy	37·7	4·6	?	99
Tubectomy	31·6			
Abortions[4]	27·5	2·5	62+	51 (2 or more abortions)

[1] Mahopatra, P. S., Central Family Planning Institute, *All-India summary of 34 studies involving 132,000 patients.*
[2] Department of Family Planning, Ministry of Health, *National study in acceptability of oral contraceptives involving 8,963 patients.*
[3] This is median parity.
[4] Confidential study of urban abortion centre based on 404 patients.

Conclusion

Data volunteered by a professional abortionist confirm the common practice in India of illegally induced abortions. The patients are characterized as married women with fewer living children than those who accept the loop and the pill, but who, in choosing this clandestine procedure under the present law, are exposed to unidentified levels of maternal morbidity and mortality.

New Delhi
26 June 1969

Appendix 5

THE POPULATION OF INDIA ACCORDING TO 1951, 1961 AND 1971 CENSUSES

Sl. No.	State/Union Territory	1951[1]	1961[1]	1971[2]
1.	Andhra Pradesh	31,115,259	35,983,447	43,394,951
2.	Assam	8,830,732	11,872,772	14,857,314
3.	Bihar	38,783,778	46,455,610	56,387,296
4.	Gujarat	16,262,657	20,633,350	26,660,929
5.	Haryana	*	*	9,971,165
6.	Jammu and Kashmir	3,253,852	3,560,976	4,615,176
7.	Kerala	13,549,118	16,903,715	21,280,397
8.	Madhya Pradesh	26,071,637	32,372,408	41,449,729
9.	Madras (Tamil Nadu)	30,119,047	33,686,953	41,103,125
10.	Maharashtra	32,002,564	39,553,718	50,295,081
11.	Mysore	19,401,956	23,586,772	29,224,046
12.	Orissa	14,645,946	17,548,846	21,934,827[3]
13.	Punjab	16,134,890	20,306,812	13,472,972
14.	Rajasthan	15,970,774	20,155,602	25,724,142
15.	Uttar Pradesh	63,215,742	73,746,401	88,299,453
16.	West Bengal	26,302,386	34,926,279	44,440,095
17.	Nagaland	212,975	369,200	515,561
18.	Andaman and Nicobar Islands	30,971	63,548	115,090
19.	Chandigarh	*	*	256,979
20.	Dadar and Nagar Haveli	41,532	57,963	74,165
21.	Delhi	1,744,072	2,658,612	4,044,338
22.	Goa, Daman and Diu	637,591	626,978	857,180
23.	Himachal Pradesh	1,109,466	1,351,144	3,424,332[3]
24.	Laccadive, Minicoy and Amindive Islands	21,035	24,108	31,798
25.	Manipur	577,635	780,037	1,069,555
26.	North East Frontier Agency	—	336,558	444,744
27.	Pondicherry	317,253	369,079	
28.	Tripura	639,029	1,142,005	1,555,822
29.	Sikkim	137,725	162,189	
30.	Other areas			
	Total	361,129,622	439,235,082	547,949,809

[1] *Census of India 1961, Paper No. 1 of 1962* (New Delhi, Government of India Press, 1962), p. 8.
[2] Census of India 1971, figures released by the Registrar-General of India in April 1971.
[3] Reorganized States.
* Included in the Punjab.

Appendix 6

THE RELIGIOUS COMPOSITION OF INDIA'S POPULATION ACCORDING TO THE 1951, 1961[1] AND 1971[2] CENSUSES

Community	Total (Millions) 1951	Per cent	Total (millions) 1961	Per cent	Total (millions) 1971	Per cent
Hindus	303·6	84·98	366·5	83·50	453·2	82·72
Muslims	35·4	9·91	46·9	10·70	61·4	11·21
Christians	8·4	2·35	10·7	2·44	14·2	2·60
Sikhs	6·2	1·74	7·8	1·79	10·3	1·89
Buddhists	0·2	0·05	3·3	0·74	3·8	0·70
Jains	1·6	0·45	2·0	0·46	2·8	0·47
Others	1·8	0·52	1·6	0·37	2·1	0·40
Religion not stated	—	—	—	—	0·27	0·01
All Communities	357·0	100·00	438·8	100·00	547·9	100·00

[1] *Census of India 1961*, vol. I, part II–C (i), social and cultural tables (New Delhi, Government of India Press, 1965), pp. 482–3.
[2] The Registrar-General's press release on the religious composition of India's population dated 20 June 1972.

Note: The total population of India according to the 1951 and 1961 censuses was 361·1 million and 439·2 million respectively. Community break-down for 3·9 million in 1951 and 0·4 million in 1961 is not available.

Appendix 7

SELECT EDITORIAL COMMENT ON ABORTION FROM
THE INDIAN PRESS

1. From the Times of India *(Bombay), 6 October 1968*

Playing with Lives

The Union Health Ministry has lately been quite active on the family planning front. But why has it been so slow in piloting a Bill in Parliament to liberalize abortions? The Shantilal Shah Committee submitted its report on the subject at the beginning of last year. It recommended that the existing law be amended to legalize abortions in certain cases, as, for instance, when the continuance of the pregnancy would gravely injure the physical or mental health of the woman. Many would argue that even these suggestions do not go far enough and that a more liberal law – similar to the one in Denmark or Sweden – is what is needed here. But the least that the Central authorities can do is to act on the Committee's somewhat modest recommendations. Yet, the Bill on the subject has been hanging fire for a long time. The Union Health Ministry has repeatedly postponed its introduction in Parliament. To a certain extent the apathy of the States is to blame. Last year they were asked to give their comments; not one of them bothered to reply. Such callous indifference is inexcusable. But the Centre cannot use it to justify its own inaction. If the States have been apathetic, the Union Health Ministry need not throw up its hands in despair. It should go ahead with the measure; family planning is, after all, on the concurrent list. According to one expert about 4 million women in the country – the vast majority of them married – undergo abortions every year. Of these, nearly 200,000 lost their lives, largely because abortions are often performed by quacks or other untrained persons. A more liberal law on abortion will not by itself solve the problem. More doctors and a better educated public are also needed. But the proposed Bill is the first essential step. Dr S. Chandrasekhar, the Union Health Minister, recently said that he intends to introduce it in the next session of Parliament. He should keep to his word. With each delay, he is only playing with people's lives.

2. From the 'Journal' of the Christian Medical Association of India (Nagpur), August 1969

Liberalization of abortion as a measure to control population

In two articles in *The Hindu* of Madras, Dr S. Chandrasekhar makes a strong plea for implementation of a more liberal policy on abortion. The subject is so important that it is worthwhile quoting his arguments and where necessary making our own comments.

> Today [says the doctor] the question of abortion is not merely a human and social problem but also a legal and medical problem. And to some

extent the humanitarian and progressive nature of a present-day government can be judged by its attitude towards abortion. Attitudes range from the permissive, as in Scandinavia and almost all the east European communist countries where legal abortion can be obtained for many pertinent reasons, to the preventive and restrictive, as in the United States of America and the Latin American countries where sometimes neither rape nor incest is considered sufficient cause for abortion.

The Report of the Abortion Committee points out:

Some guesses can be made on the magnitude of the problem. If it is assumed that for every 73 live births 25 abortions take place of which 15 are induced, the number of abortions annually in a 1,000 population may be approximately 13·5 natural and 8 induced (corresponding to the estimated birth rate of 39). In a population of 500 million the number of abortions per year will be 6·5 million, 3·9 million natural and 2·6 million induced. As for the total cost of abortion, the Committee observes, 'Assuming an average expenditure of Rs 50 per induced abortion, the annual expenditure on induced abortions may be Rs 19·5 crores.'

It is surmised that a very large percentage of abortions in India are among married women. Section 312 of the IPC lays down that: 'Whoever voluntarily causes a woman with child to miscarry shall, if such miscarriage be not caused in good faith for the purpose of saving the life of the woman, be punished with imprisonment of either description for a term which may extend to seven years and shall also be liable to a fine.'

In Great Britain, however, the law has been amended. The 1967 amended British law includes the statement:

A person shall not be guilty of an offence under the law relating to abortion when a pregnancy is terminated by a registered medical practitioner if two registered medical practitioners are of the opinion formed in good faith:
a. That the continuance of the pregnancy would involve risk to the life of the pregnant woman or any existing children of her family, greater than if the pregnancy were terminated, or
b. That there is a substantial risk that if the child were born it would suffer from such physical or mental abnormalities as to be seriously handicapped.

In determining whether the continuance of a pregnancy would involve such risk of injury to health as is mentioned in paragraph (a) of the sub-section 1 of this section, account may be taken of the pregnant woman's actual or foreseeable environment.

In India, however, Section 312 of the IPC remains unchanged. A large proportion of women who resort to abortion, the law being as it is, are forced to go to quacks or unscrupulous doctors and morbidity and even mortality following such interference are necessarily high. Statistics are hard to get as these cases are not reported to the police as both the parties concerned are afraid of prosecution. It is this sheer futile wastage of precious human lives that has made the medical profession and the general public demand that the question of illegal abortion be reviewed and re-examined as a whole.

The learned doctor says: 'A law which rigidly prohibits something which nevertheless continues as a fairly widespread practice in the community is one that requires re-examination and change, if necessary. Law is the vehicle of society. Therefore, the question how far permitted abortions can serve the wider purposes of family and of society can bear dispassionate examination.'

While one may agree to the above argument, one cannot but ask why the Government sticks to the Prohibition Policy, or the Gold control order, as these prohibitive laws too deal with something which nevertheless continues as a fairly widespread practice in the community and therefore might require re-examination and change, if necessary. However, this is a parenthetical passing thought.

The Government of India in the Central Ministry of Health and Family Planning, evincing deep concern with this state of affairs, appointed the Shantilal Shah Committee. in 1964. Its recommendations as amended below were presented to the Government for adoption:

> The Committee considers the above (Section 312 IPC) provision too restrictive and, therefore, recommends that it be liberalized to allow termination of pregnancy by a qualified medical practitioner acting in good faith not only for saving the pregnant woman's life but also:
> When the continuance of the pregnancy would involve serious risk to the life, or grave injury to the health, whether physical or mental, of the pregnant woman, whether before, at, or after the birth; or
> Provided the woman or her husband undergoes voluntary sterilization to ward off the danger of repeated abortions and further pregnancies except in cases where under exceptional circumstances such sterilization is not considered necessary by the authorized medical practitioner carrying out the termination of pregnancy.

Illustrations

   a. If a couple has been using family planning devices for the purposes of planning their family, and if a pregnancy occurs as a result of failure of such devices, the anguish arising from the continuance of an unwanted pregnancy may constitute a grave injury to the mental health of the pregnant woman;
   b. When there is a substantial risk that if the child were born it would suffer from such physical or mental abnormalities as to be seriously handicapped in life; or
   c. When the pregnancy results from rape, intercourse with an unmarried girl under the age of 16 or intercourse with a mentally defective woman.

A differentiation is sought to be made in the procedure for termination of pregnancy within three months and later. In the former case a registered medical practitioner is authorized to perform the operation while after the pregnancy has gone beyond three months a second medical opinion is considered essential.

To quote:

> The treatment must be carried out in a place for the time being approved for the purpose, by the Government of India or the State Government. The opinion and second opinion, as the case may be, must be certified in writing by the practitioner who carried out the termination of pregnancy before the treatment is begun.
>
> There must have been before treatment a consent in writing by the pregnant woman, or, if under 18 years of age, the pregnant girl and one of her parents or of the pregnant girl and her guardian for the termination of the pregnancy.
>
> Provided that where the practitioner is of the opinion formed in good faith, that the termination is immediately necessary in order to save the life of the pregnant woman (and certifies his opinion in writing either before or after carrying out the treatment) the above conditions need not be complied with.

The Committee, while making the above recommendations, also strongly recommends that:

a. In order to prevent the danger of repeated abortions in the case of women who are not fit to bear the strain of further pregnancies, the medical practitioner should advise the woman and/or her husband to undergo voluntary sterilization.
b. The idea of a small family norm achieved through control of conception should be vigorously promoted.
c. Readily accessible services for family planning should be extended.
d. Family life education to develop healthy and responsible attitudes towards sex, marriage and parenthood should be promoted.

As a result of further consultations a Bill has been placed before the Parliament titled *The Medical Termination of Pregnancy Bill, 1969*.

The *illustrations* given above by the Committee permit termination of pregnancy if a couple due to failure of family planning devices is faced with an unwanted pregnancy. This is placing a premium on carelessness, and to say that such unwanted pregnancy may constitute a grave injury to the mental health of the pregnant woman is, I am afraid, just begging the question:

> It is my personal belief [says Dr Chandrasekhar], that any woman in our country, at any time, should be able to obtain a legal abortion from a public or a private clinic without giving any reason. We have come a long way in emancipating our women but the evolution of their emancipation cannot be complete unless we grant them the right not to have a baby they do not want. I cannot understand with what grace men can deny women this right.
>
> Secondly, we must examine abortion from the point of view of the unborn child who may be physically deformed or mentally retarded, and

the unwanted normal child who becomes the unloved and uncared for child and in time the delinquent child. The problems here are too obvious to need comment, especially in view of the daily newspaper evidence of the growing incidence of delinquent behaviour of children and teenagers.

Everyone will not agree that any woman should be at liberty to ask for an abortion without any real reason, from the social or health point of view. Also, how is one to foresee the birth of a deformed baby or one which might develop to be a delinquent? This seems to be a totally wrong way of looking at the problem.

There is no doubt that from the point of view of the State and Society and the total demographic picture the problem is really very urgent. While abortion need not be considered a valid method of family planning, despite the experience of Japan, the demographic aspect of abortion merits some consideration and one will easily agree with the Minister in this. He further adduces the following argument.

The magnitude and the pressing nature of our population problem is too well known to need any detailed repetition. India ranks second in the world in population numbers and seventh in respect of land area. With an area of only 2·4 per cent of the total land area of the world, she has to support about 14 per cent of the world's total population, which enjoys only 1·5 per cent of the total world income. Today, India's population is about 525 million and we add to this number 13 million – an Australia – every year. At the present annual rate of growth of 2·5 per cent we shall double our population in the next 30 years and become more than a billion by the end of this century. The prospect is frightening in view of our present poor stage of economic and social development. Hence, India's avowed objective of reducing the nation's birth rate from its present 40 per 1,000 per year to 25 if not 20 as soon as possible. India has embarked on the largest official family planning programme of its kind anywhere in the world. And while I believe abortion has no role to play as a family planning method, it has a twin role in our democratic, positive, anti-natalist population policy.

A liberalized or legalized policy of abortion will not only prevent the arrival of unwanted children; what is equally if not more important, it will prevent the death of thousands of mothers every year. These mothers risk mutilation or death by seeking illegal abortion at the hands of quacks who operate furtively under the most unhygienic conditions.

Dr Chandrasekhar concludes:

Let us not forget that we can force a woman to have a child but we cannot force her to want or love one. As the distinguished American biologist, Dr Garrett Hardin, points out: 'In this day of population explosion, society has no reason to encourage the birth of more children, but it has a tremendous interest in encouraging the birth of more wanted children. Critics of abortion generally see it as an exclusively negative thing, a means of non-fulfilment only. What they fail to realize is that abortion, like other means of birth control, can lead to fulfilment in the life of a woman. A woman who aborts this year because she is in poor health, neurotic, economically harassed, unmarried, on the verge of divorce, or immature may well decide to have a child five years from now—a wanted child. The child that she aborts is always an unwanted child. If her need for abortion is frustrated she may never know the joy of a wanted child.'

The problem of adopting *abortion* as an effective method of population control bristles with many difficulties. As in the case of prohibition where we have total prohibitionists, temperance advocates and those who would have free flow of liquor, here also we have those who see eye to eye with H. H. the Pope in his encyclical, others who would only countenance family planning methods but would not interfere with pregnancy once started and, of course, those who would like to have permission to terminate unwanted pregnancies.

Conscientious Christian doctors and Christian hospitals, while being willing to deal with cases where there are real therapeutic indications, will long hesitate to interfere with pregnancy just for the social factors enumerated above. The problem is not only social but has religious implications which cannot be thrown overboard.

J. C. David (MD, FRCS)

3. From 'The Pioneer' (*Lucknow, Uttar Pradesh*), *20 November 1969*

Abortion—the Lesser Evil

Prejudices die hard. Traditional and religious quarters can, therefore, be counted upon to raise a hue and cry over the Bill seeking to liberalize abortion introduced by the Union Minister of State for Health, Dr S. Chandrasekhar, in Rajya Sabha on Monday. Yet the legislation aims at nothing more than legalizing, with rigid safeguards, a practice which is already widely prevalent in this country. Whatever the moral feelings loudly professed by society, a large number of mothers are prepared not only to risk prosecution but their very lives by resorting to illegal abortions. It is estimated that despite the present stringent law, no less than 4,000,000 illegal abortions are carried out annually. Even when done under proper medical supervision, abortion is a first class risk; when carried out by quacks in unhygienic conditions, the mortality rate is well over 50 per cent. The fact that it may help to save the lives of 2 million women every year is ample justification for the proposed legislation.

Not all critics of the measure will, however, use ethical or moral arguments. Some may, for instance, point to Japan's plight where indiscriminate abortions have depleted the population to a point where the country is threatened with acute manpower shortage. Others may cite the case of the United Kingdom where abortions are treated as routine. Not only is there no stigma attached but excellent hospital facilities are provided which draw cases from far and near, earning for London the doubtful distinction of being dubbed as the 'abortion capital of Europe'. There is, however, no basis for the fear that the proposed bill will open the floodgates of abortion in this country. For one thing, social taboos are there to discourage resort to unwarranted abortions. In clandestine abortions, such inhibitions naturally do not come into play. Moreover, the built-in restrictions in the bill are stringent enough to check its abuse.

The present law on abortion is a British legacy. Enacted over a hundred years back, it makes abortion a crime for which both the mother and the abortionist could be punished except when carried out to save the life of the mother. After careful study, the Shantilal Shah Committee has proposed amendment of the law to allow termination of pregnancy by a qualified doctor acting in good faith not only to save the mother's life but also where her health might be endangered either before or after pregnancy. Other justificatory circumstances urged by the Committee include risk of physical or mental abnormalities in the child, pregnancy as a result of rape and mental deficiency in the mother. The new legislation by and large follows the recommendation of the Shah Committee. It will be far less permissive than the laws in the United States, the United Kingdom and Japan where abortion is permitted even for specified social and economic reasons.

Medical opinion in India, despite its orthodoxy, has come out in support of liberalization of the abortion law. The President of the Indian Medical Association, Dr G. S. Wagle, even argues that 'if giving birth is the birthright of a woman, it should be her fundamental right to abort at will'. This, of course, is going too far. The considerations behind the Bill are purely humanitarian. Strictly speaking, what is envisaged is not abortion but 'medical termination of pregnancy'. Nor is the Bill intended to promote family planning – for which a separate legislation raising the marriage age of girls from 16 to 18 is to be introduced. Legislation of abortion will lead to the saving of countless lives by ensuring that such operations are carried out with the help of the latest scientific and medical techniques and in the early stages of pregnancy when the risk is relatively low. Confronted as we are with a *fait accompli*, the ethical and moral implications of abortion have ceased to be relevant. All that can be done now is to make the best of a bad job.

4. *From* 'The Searchlight' (*Patna, Bihar*), *23 November 1969*

Liberalization of Abortion Law

For quite some time now there has been new thinking on the subject of abortion law. A more liberal and realistic approach is being urged on a subject with which are mingled issues of social, economic and moral import. Birth control, to which many sections of society still take serious objection on the ground that it is immoral and against the law of nature, has very much become a fact of modern life in this country today. But even in such an advanced country like Britain in the later Victorian era the very idea of birth control was looked down upon with extreme horror and revulsion. The social conscience was shocked by what it regarded as the dirty talk of the radicals. It has gone on record that Lord Amberly, father of Bertrand Russell, had to lose his seat in Parliament because he was an advocate of birth control and women's suffrage. But today in England birth control and law on abortion have been liberalized. There should be no question of moral shock or surprise if in India also there is thinking on similar lines.

The bill seeking to liberalize abortion was introduced in the Rajya Sabha on Monday. It seeks to terminate pregnancy on health and humanitarian grounds. Abortion is also sought to be allowed in case there is fear that the child may suffer from deformities and disease. Abortion at one time was thought to be a heinous crime. In large sections of the society that outlook still prevails. We have to note that society, whether in this country or elsewhere, is male dominated and as such is liable to be unfair to its weaker section. The male escapes the burden of responsibility for his frivolities while if conception takes place it is the female who suffers and cannot even hide her condition. The consequences of share in guilt are unequal. Even otherwise the female should have a right to decide whether she would like to bear all the physical and mental agony of pregnancy and have a child or not. It may be because of her health it may be unwise for a mother to have pregnancy. Childbirth may even endanger her life. Surely in such cases the safety and health of the mother should be the deciding factor and abortion should be allowed. There is an equally strong case if there is apprehension, from family history or otherwise, that the child born may be deformed.

It is estimated that per thousand of population in this country there are 13 abortions, and out of these 5 are natural and 8 are induced. Which would, in other words, mean that in a population of 50 crores there are per year about 65 lakh abortions—26 lakh natural and 39 lakh induced. This only reveals the size of the problem, even though these data are inadequate and cannot give the full picture. However, the consequences of the liberalization of the abortion law have also to be borne in mind. In Japan, the only country in Asia that has moulded its life to the Western pattern, registered abortions rose from 11·8 per thousand women of child-bearing age in 1949 to a peak of 50·2 per thousand in 1955 following legalization of abortion. In the eastern European countries also, like Hungary and Bulgaria, abortions have shot up. In 1960–1, there were 139 abortions as against 100 births in Hungary; in Bulgaria the figure was 58 per 100 births.

Naturally great care is to be taken in changing the abortion law. We cannot be very liberal with the liberalization. In the first instance, medical facilities are not adequate enough to meet the needs of a liberalized abortion law. There is great danger that quacks and the unscrupulous elements in the medical profession would take advantage of undue liberalization, as they have done in family planning. Besides, in the absence of sufficient educational awareness society cannot yet go in for a truly liberalized abortion law. But there is no reason why a fair measure of benefits of a liberal abortion law should not be made available in difficult cases. No harm will be done to society, and it will make all the difference for the happiness and wellbeing of the individual families concerned. Much would depend on the final form the law takes. It is for the members of Parliament to see that the law they frame does not leave loopholes for malpractices to grow.

5. From the 'Eastern Economist' (New Delhi), 5 December 1969

Abortion Law: Half-Hearted

In the socio-economic context in which the government has introduced the Medical Termination of Pregnancy Bill, 1969, in Rajya Sabha, the provisions of this proposed legislation are bound to be scrutinized in terms of their bearing on the national programme of family planning and population control. The Statement of Objects and Reasons, however, refrains from mentioning population control as one of the purposes which the Bill has in view. This seems to us to be a pointless exercise in diplomatic evasion. Whether the government likes it or not this Bill will certainly be debated in terms of its relevance to the nation's family planning effort which is also a definite government policy and programme.

Not that the more openly avowed objects of the Bill are of secondary importance. The cross of an unwanted or enforced pregnancy is certainly too outrageous a burden to be imposed on its women by any society claiming to be civilized. There could therefore be wholehearted acceptance of the declared purpose of the Bill, which is to liberalize certain existing provisions in the Indian Penal Code relating to termination of pregnancy, these liberalizations being conceived '(1) as a health measure – when there is a danger to the life or risk to physical or mental health of the woman; (2) on humanitarian grounds – such as when pregnancy arises from a sex crime like rape or intercourse with a lunatic woman etc.; and (3) eugenic grounds – where there is substantial risk that the child, if born, would suffer from deformities and diseases'.

In justifying the legalization, along liberal lines, of the termination of unwanted or enforced pregnancies on the grounds mentioned in the Statement of Objects and Reasons attached to the Bill, the government is certainly in an unassailable position. Although under the existing law abortion is a crime for which the mother as well as the abortionist could be punished, the brutal fact of life as it is lived is that a large number of illegal abortions do take place. Thanks to the fact that such abortions involve a violation of law, they are often performed by medical unqualified personnel in clandestine circumstances which greatly aggravate the risk to life or health of the woman so treated. In the Statement of Objects and Reasons it is pointed out that, in recent years, with health services having expanded and hospitals being availed of to the increasing extent by all classes of society, 'doctors have often been confronted with gravely ill or dying pregnant women whose pregnant uterus (sic) have been tampered with, with a view to causing an abortion and consequently suffered very severely'. We may perhaps quarrel with the grammar of this observation, but we must accept its substance and truth.

In the nature of things, there could only be informed speculation about the extent of this particular evil. That it is prevalent fairly widely is, however, evident enough. The government therefore has not only the right but is also under an obligation to give legal sanction as well as provide medical facilities for the termination of unwanted or enforced pregnancies on the health, humanitarian or eugenic grounds mentioned in the Statement of Objects and Reasons.

The main operative provisions of the Bill provide for the legislation of abortions where '(1) the continuance of the pregnancy would involve a risk to the life of the pregnant woman or of injury to her physical or mental health; or (2) there is a substantial risk that if the child were born, it would suffer from such physical or mental abnormalities as to be seriously handicapped'. These passages in the Bill meet its aim of providing for the termination of pregnancies as a health measure, on humanitarian grounds or for eugenic considerations. But as we had said earlier the Bill must also be studied in terms of its possible contribution to the population control programme. Here, Explanations (i) and (ii) appended to sub-section (2) of Section 3 of the Bill become relevant, or rather Explanation (ii) has to be taken particular note of. Thus, while Explanation (i) provides that 'where any pregnancy is alleged by the pregnant women to have been caused by rape, the anguish caused by such pregnancy shall be presumed to constitute a grave injury to the mental health of the pregnant woman'. Explanation (ii) prescribes that 'where any pregnancy occurs as a result of failure of any device used by any married woman or her husband for the purpose of limiting the number of children, the anguish caused by such unwanted pregnancy may be presumed to constitute a grave injury to the mental health of the pregnant woman'.

Thus, although the government has been reluctant to put forward this Bill as a substantial measure of population control, it has still made some provision for legalized abortion being availed of by pregnant women for the purpose of limiting the number of children provided it could be shown that these women have a history of using contraceptive devices. The object here, apparently, is to establish the 'unwanted nature' of the pregnancy in question. There will, of course, be more than one opinion on the necessity or desirability of the abundant caution displayed by the Bill in liberalizing the abortion law in terms of the purpose of limiting the number of children.

That the government is, to some extent, anxious to allow for the resort of abortion to become a means of limitation of families is clear enough. If, nevertheless, it has hesitated to present this legalization openly as a direct measure of family planning, it must be because it believes that public opinion is not yet ripe for an advance of this kind. Even so, this part of the Bill, as it stands, is decidedly unsatisfactory. Take, for instance, the reference to failure of contraceptive 'devices or techniques'. Not every contraceptive technique necessarily involes the use of a 'device'. There is the rhythm method, for what it is worth, and there is also the practice of *coitus interruptus*. The adoption of one or the other of these techniques does indicate, surely, a desire on the part of the couple concerned to avoid the woman becoming pregnant. A pregnancy taking place in such circumstances would therefore clearly be an unwanted pregnancy. Why should the benefit of the abortion Bill be denied in such cases simply because no contraceptive devices as such have been used by the couple concerned?

This is an obvious flaw in the Bill in its present form. In our view, the reference to the use of a contraceptive 'device' should be dropped and the term 'device' may be replaced by the more comprehensive term 'technique'. It is also desirable that the law should stipulate that all that should be required of the women in these cases is a simple declaration that they did want to avoid a pregnancy and had taken whatever precautions they knew of or could employ for the purpose.

Some of us may perhaps like to go even further. If all that the law intends is that there should be reasonable ground for presuming that a pregnancy is an unwanted one – and we believe that the law should not demand more than this – it should be possible for an abortion to be legally sanctioned on request in all those cases where a woman already has three children or has had her last child within the previous twenty-four months. It is our view that the possibility or the importance of obscurantist opposition to such further liberalizations of the abortion law could be exaggerated. In any case, after having rightly ventured so far, the government clearly owes it to itself to encourage any tendency that there may be for non-official amendments to be moved on the lines we have suggested here so that the proposed Bill could play an effective part in furthering the national policy of population control and the government's programme of family planning.

6. From the 'Tribune' (Ambala, Punjab), 6 December 1969

Abortion Law

Commending the Bill for liberalization of the existing law on abortions, Dr Chandrasekhar said that 6·5 million abortions are taking place in India every year – 3·9 million being induced abortions. He did not say how he arrived at these figures. The Shantilal Shah Committee which reported on the question three years ago said: 'Statistics on abortion are difficult to evaluate, particularly because of the difficulty in collecting information. As it is still an illegal activity, no records are available of either the operation or its after-effects. Hence there are likely to be gross errors of estimation of the extent of mortality or other untoward consequences of illegal abortions. It is difficult to get a realistic estimate of the ratio of induced abortions to spontaneous or therapeutic abortions.' The figures given by Dr Chandrasekhar, both of total abortions and of the ratio of induced abortions, cannot therefore go unchallenged. It is unfortunate that the demand for circulating the bill for eliciting public opinion did not find much favour in the House. It was said that the Bill had already been discussed with the State Governments and social welfare organizations. As Mrs Shakuntala Paranjpye pointed out, though the Shantilal Shah Committee had issued the questionnaire to all MPs, only nine of them replied to it. There can be little doubt that a measure of such far-reaching consequences would only have gained – and not lost anything – by public discussion before it was enacted.

Japan is cited as a striking illustration of a country which has reduced its birth rate by legalizing abortions. There are also some other countries where the birth rate is alleged to have fallen as a consequence of legalizing abortions. But the UN *Demographic Year Book* has a different story to tell. It says that the east European countries which have legalized abortions have witnessed an increase in the totals of births and abortions. Termination of pregnancy made it possible for the woman to conceive again earlier than would have been possible otherwise: 'Legalization, by increasing the total number of abortions, has thus resulted in an increased number of conceptions.' The spread of contraceptive practices has also not led to any drop in the incidence of abortions. It is precisely in those countries where contraceptive knowledge is freely disseminated that the largest number of abortions take place.

According to Dr Chandrasekhar, liberalization is being sought on three counts – as a health measure, as a humanitarian gesture when sex crimes and lunatic women were involved, and as eugenic measure to prevent the birth of deformed children. Mr Raj Narain who supported the Bill found these reasons rather unconvincing. He said that it would have been far better for the Minister to say simply that in the conditions of today legalization of abortion has become necessary. The necessity is not so self-evident, although Mrs Pushpa Mehta recounted the story of how even Vishwamitra did not accept his baby daughter, Shakuntala, born of Menaka, to illustrate the plight of the woman who had the misfortune to conceive out of wedlock. If the Shantilal Shah Committee is correct, induced abortion as a means of terminating unwanted pregnancies has existed 'ever since ancient times'. The true moral of the Menaka story could well be that abortions have been viewed in India with abhorrence even from ancient times, and that the present attempts to make them legal and respectable may be somewhat misconceived.

From the 'Nagpur Times' (*Nagpur*), *18 December 1969*

Liberalization of Abortion

The Indian society has been so steeped in tradition and orthodoxy that it generally views with disfavour any reformation that departs from the routine; more so when it has a semblance of moral aspect. The opposition that the Abortion Bill is encountering presently stems from this traditional attitude. But the complexities of modern life have given rise to such complex problems that their solutions become impossible if the traditional attitude is not rationalized.

The issue of abortion is one such problem. The Indian Penal Code views abortion as a crime punishable with imprisonment except when the miscarriage is caused for the purpose of saving the life of a woman. This law was devised hundred years ago in line with the British law of the time. But during this period of hundred years the societies in different countries have undergone a total transformation, creating a host of problems for every succeeding generation with phenomenal rise in populations. With these changes, strict abortion laws have also been substantially liberalized in most Western countries. India cannot choose to lag far behind.

Even with the strictness of the abortion law as enshrined in the Indian Penal Code, it is no secret that the provision has all along been breached with impunity in both rural and urban areas. According to one estimate, 50 lakh illegal abortions are performed in the country every year as against 2 crore live births. Quacks are believed to kill 2 lakh mothers every year through clandestine abortions. A large number of women are prepared to risk their lives in an illegal abortion rather than go through normal child birth. This being the situation, eminent public men including doctors demanded a review of the question of abortions and in deference to this demand, the Centre appointed a committee in 1964, under the chairmanship of Mr Shantilal Shah, a former Minister in Maharashtra, to review the law relating to abortions.

The Shantilal Shah Committee, after examining all aspects of the question concluded that sound reasons exist for revising the existing law. The Committee, which submitted its report two years ago, has observed that whatever may be the moral and ethical feelings that are professed by the society as a whole on the question of induced abortion, it is an incontrovertible fact that large numbers of mothers are prepared to risk their lives in an illegal abortion rather than carry the particular child to term. The Committee recommended termination of pregnancy by a qualified medical practitioner not only for saving the pregnant woman's life but also (1) when continuance of pregnancy would involve serious risk to the life or grave injury to the physical or mental health of the pregnant woman; (2) when there is a substantial risk that if the child were born, it would suffer from serious physical or mental abnormalities; or (3) when pregnancy has resulted from rape or intercourse with an unmarried girl under 16 or intercourse with a mentally defective woman.

Most orthodox opposition to these measures stemmed from the feeling that abortion was a means 'to destroy or rather kill human life even if it be in the womb'. But even among women, there have been strong supporters of abortion. A woman M.P., criticizing those who saw corruption and immorality in everything, said, 'If liberalization of abortion can lead to corruption, so can all other family planning methods.' The Secretary to the Union Health Ministry told newsmen two years ago that illegal abortions were carried out in the country on a large scale resulting in great misery and numerous deaths. 'Our hospitals are getting a large number of unsuccessful spoilt abortions every day,' he said, and added, 'When our women are so desperate as to risk their lives, should the Government and society ignore it?'

Abortion has to be viewed more as a human problem than as a moral or a population problem. Besides treating abortion as a 'health measure', the Bill does cover 'humanitarian' grounds such as when pregnancy arises from a sex crime or in a lunatic woman but does not seem to take into account the case of unmarried girls contracting pregnancy through 'human folly'. In Hindu society particularly, begetting a child in an unmarried status attaches a stigma which the girl has to carry through the length of her life. Such a girl becomes a social outcast and not one noble soul comes forward to retrieve her from calumny by offering to marry her. Having no courage to face social derision, unmarried girls contracting pregnancy resort to any means to get rid of the unwanted child and imperil their lives or end their agony by ending their own lives. Such cases have to be treated as coming under 'humanitarian grounds' and special provisions are needed to ensure that their cases are disposed of 'confidentially'. If such an unfortunate girl approaches a qualified physician for 'deliverance', there need be no procedural hurdles which may be necessary in other categories of cases.

Anyway, the Union Government has taken a bold step in introducing the Bill which was long overdue. The measure is essentially one designed to liberalize the abortion law and not one to universally legalize induced abortion as in Japan. Probably either Japan's experiment is indiscriminate or that country is 100 years ahead of the rest of the world. So far as India is concerned, the rationalization measure has been a dire necessity of the day and the Centre has done well in putting the necessary foot forward. Not only this, the Union Minister Dr. Chandrasekhar has gone one step ahead by announcing that a 'suction pump' which is in use in the Soviet Union to terminate pregnancy would be locally manufactured and put to use in India. That shows Government's desire to implement the measure with will and determination.

7. From the 'Amrit Bazar Patrika' (*Calcutta*), *1 January 1970*

Rootless Topic

A panel discussion held recently at the India International Centre, New Delhi, expressed itself overwhelmingly in favour of liberalizing laws dealing with abortion. It is indeed a case of modernism with vengeance. While responsible methods are open to the people for limiting the family, there is no reason why a negative and potentially dangerous formula should be made use of with the sanction of law. Of course, it may be a step in saving pregnant women who do not want children to be born to them from the clutches of quacks. A statutory provision would no doubt entitle them to the care of competent medical advice. But it almost amounts to inflicting a wound and bothering to heal it later, when it might be too late in some cases. The fact that there are 6,500,000 abortion cases in India every year, does not necessarily justify liberalization that would uphold a practice that is not necessary and against tradition. The proposed Bill in Parliament, however, views the problem in proper perspective and seeks to limit abortion only on medical, eugenic and humanitarian grounds. Seen from this angle, the whole discussion of the Panel may be reasonably dismissed as a 'rootless topic', as a speaker so aptly described. The ideal method would be to stress on responsible parenthood.

The suggestion has been made that legal abortion is the only answer to clandestine methods. While there is a point in this kind of thinking, it is necessary to stress that this would invariably encourage profligacy. The experience of Japan, where abortion was accepted as a part of progressive social attitude, has not been a happy one and it has little to inspire others. In England, two doctors have to agree in 'good faith' before a pregnancy can be terminated, according to the provisions of the Abortion Act. And as Jane McKerron, writing in the columns of the *New Statesman*, observes: 'The anti-reform lobby appear to be continually haunted by the spectre of unscrupulous doctors twisting their faith to their financial advantage.' She also admits that this does occur and is *unavoidable*. One hardly anticipates such a bending of faith, at least in England. Judging by the experiences of the past in the matter of widespread abuse of the law, there could be reasonable apprehension that the Abortion Law would fare no better in India.

Shorn of all conflicting and confusing verdicts on the issue, there is ample necessity for viewing the problem in a straightforward manner. Abortion should be permitted essentially on ethical and humanitarian grounds and not on other pleas. The permissive society is yet to grow in India. The disinclination to destroy life in its very initial stage is reported to be an evidence of the influence of inhibition, as modernists would perhaps claim. But in reality, the introduction of abortion would be an unnecessary exercise to remove the after-effects of 'pleasure unlimited'. The recognized forms of birth control are not that unreliable. The recent report about some one dying as a result of taking the pill may be true in all its contents. But this does not necessarily prove that it is plainly inefficacious. An effort to terminate pregnancy may also equally result in disaster. Above all, the move might have far-reaching repercussions on Indian society.

Appendix 8

UNITED STATES SUPREME COURT DECISIONS IN TEXAS AND
GEORGIA ABORTION CASES

1

On 22 January 1973 the United States Supreme Court decided two abortion cases: (1) the 'Texas' case (*Roe* v. *Wade*)[1] and (2) the 'Georgia' case (*Doe* v. *Bolton*).[2] Both decisions were by a majority of 7 to 2, with Justice Blackmun writing the majority opinions.

We reproduce below for lack of space only the syllabus of both decisions and not the text of the decisions themselves. (A Syllabus is prepared by the Reporter of Decisions of the Supreme Court and is released as a headnote with the Decision for the convenience of the reader. The Syllabus constitutes no part of the opinion of the Court as such.)

Roe et al. v. Wade, District Attorney of Dallas County

A pregnant single woman (Roe) brought a class action challenging the constitutionality of the Texas criminal abortion laws, which proscribe procuring or attempting an abortion except on medical advice for the purpose of saving the mother's life. A licensed physician (Hallford), who had two state abortion prosecutions pending against him, was permitted to intervene. A childless married couple (the Does), the wife not being pregnant, separately attacked the laws, basing alleged injury on the future possibilities of contraceptive failure, pregnancy, unpreparedness for parenthood, and impairment of the wife's health. A three-judge District Court, which consolidated the actions, held that Roe and Hallford, and members of their classes, had standing to sue and presented justiciable controversies. Ruling that declaratory, though not injunctive, relief was warranted, the court declared the abortion statutes void as vague and overbroadly infringing those plaintiffs' Ninth and Fourteenth Amendment rights. The court ruled the Does' complaint not justiciable. Appellants directly appealed to this Court on the injunctive rulings, and appellee cross-appealed from the District Court's grant of declaratory relief to Roe and Hallford. *Held:*

1. While 28 U. S. C. § 1253 authorizes no direct appeal to this Court from the grant or denial of declaratory relief alone, review is not foreclosed when the case is properly before the Court on appeal from specific denial of injunctive relief and the arguments as to both injunctive and declaratory relief are necessarily identical. P. 8.

2. Roe has standing to sue; the Does and Hallford do not. Pp. 9–14.

(a) Contrary to appellee's contention, the natural termination of Roe's pregnancy did not moot her suit. Litigation involving pregnancy, which is

---

[1] US Supreme Court: *Roe et al.* v. *Wade*, District Attorney of Dallas County, 41 *Law Weekly* 4213 (Decision dated 22 January 1973).
[2] US Supreme Court: *Doe et al.* v. *Bolton, Attorney General et al.*, 41 *Law Weekly* 4233 (Decision dated 22 January 1973).

'capable of repetition, yet evading review', is an exception to the usual federal rule that an actual controversy must exist at review stages and not simply when the action is initiated. Pp. 9–10.

(b) The District Court correctly refused injunctive, but erred in granting declaratory relief to Hallford, who alleged no federally protected right not assertable as a defence against the good-faith state prosecutions pending against him. *Samuels* v. *Mackell*, 401 US 66.

(c) The Does' complaint, based as it is on contingencies, any one or more of which may not occur, is too speculative to present an actual case or controversy. Pp. 12–14.

3. State criminal abortion laws, like those involved here, that except from criminality only a life-saving procedure on the mother's behalf without regard to the stage of her pregnancy and other interests involved violate the Due Process Clause of the Fourteenth Amendment, which protects against state action the right to privacy, including a woman's qualified right to terminate her pregnancy. Though the State cannot override that right, it has legitimate interests in protecting both the pregnant woman's health and the potentiality of human life, each of which interests grows and reaches a 'compelling' point at various stages of the woman's approach to term. Pp. 36–49.

(a) For the stage prior to approximately the end of the first trimester, the abortion decision and its effectuation must be left to the medical judgment of the pregnant woman's attending physician. Pp. 36–47.

(b) For the stage subsequent to approximately the end of the first trimester, the State, in promoting its interest in the health of the mother, may, if it chooses, regulate the abortion procedure in ways that are reasonably related to maternal health. Pp. 43–4.

(c) For the stage subsequent to viability the State, in promoting its interest in the potentiality of human life, may, if it chooses, regulate, and even proscribe, abortion except where necessary, in appropriate medical judgement, for the preservation of the life or health of the mother. Pp. 44–8.

4. The State may define the term 'physician' to mean only a physician currently licensed by the State, and may proscribe any abortion by a person who is not a physician as so defined. Pp. 34–5, 48.

5. It is unnecessary to decide the injunctive relief issue since the Texas authorities will doubtless fully recognize the Court's ruling that the Texas criminal abortion statutes are unconstitutional. P. 51.

314 F. Supp. 1217, affirmed in part and reversed in part.

Blackmun, J., delivered the opinion of the Court, in which Burger, C. J., and Douglas, Brennan, Stewart, Marshall, and Powell, J-J., joined. Burger, C. J., and Douglas and Stewart, J-J., filed concurring opinions. White, J., filed a dissenting opinion, in which Rehnquist, J., joined. Rehnquist, J., filed a dissenting opinion.

Doe et al. v. Bolton, Attorney General of Georgia, et al.

Georgia law proscribes an abortion except as performed by a duly licensed Georgia physician when necessary in 'his best clinical judgement 'because continued pregnancy would endanger a pregnant woman's life or injure her health; the foetus would likely be born with serious defects; or the pregnancy resulted from rape. § 26-1202 (a) of Ga. Criminal Code. In addition to a requirement that the patient be a Georgia resident and certain other requirements, the statutory scheme poses three procedural conditions in § 26-1202 (b): (1) that the abortion be performed in a hospital accredited by the Joint Committee on Accreditation of Hospitals (JCAH); (2) that the procedure be approved by the hospital staff abortion committee; and (3) that the performing physician's judgement be confirmed by independent examinations of the patient by two other licensed physicians. Appellant Doe, an indigent married Georgia citizen, who was denied an abortion after eight weeks of pregnancy for failure to meet any of the § 26-1202 (a) conditions, sought declaratory and injunctive relief, contending that the Georgia laws were unconstitutional. Others joining in the complaint included Georgia-licensed physicians (who claimed that the Georgia statutes 'chilled and deterred' their practices), registered nurses, clergymen, and social workers. Though holding that all the plaintiffs had standing, the District Court ruled that only Doe presented a justiciable controversy. In Doe's case the Court gave declaratory, but not injunctive, relief, invalidating as an infringement of privacy and personal liberty the limitation to the three situations specified in § 26-1202 (a) and certain other provisions but holding that the State's interest in health protection and the existence of a *'potential* of independent human existence' justified regulation through § 26-1202 (b) of the 'manner of performance as well as the quality of the final decision to abort'. The appellants, claiming entitlement to broader relief, directly appealed to this Court. *Held:*

1. Doe's case presents a live, justiciable controversy and she has standing to sue, *Roe* v. *Wade, ante*, p. —, as do the physician-appellants (who, unlike the physician in *Wade*, were not charged with abortion violations), and it is therefore unnecessary to resolve the issue of the other appellants' standing. Pp. 7-9.

2. A woman's constitutional right to an abortion is not absolute. *Roe* v. *Wade, supra*. P. 9.

3. The requirement that a physician's decision to perform an abortion must rest upon 'his best clinical judgement' of its necessity is not unconstitutionally vague, since that judgement may be made in the light of *all* the attendant circumstances. *United States* v. *Vuitch*, 402 US 62, 71-2. Pp. 10-12.

4. The three procedural conditions in § 26-1202 (b) violate the Fourteenth Amendment. Pp. 12-19.

(a) The JCAH accreditation requirement is invalid, since the State has not shown that only hospitals (let alone those with JCAH accreditation) meet its interest in fully protecting the patient; and a hospital requirement failing to exclude the first trimester of pregnancy would be invalid on that ground alone, see *Roe* v. *Wade, supra*. Pp. 12-15.

(b) The interposition of a hospital committee on abortion, a procedure not applicable as a matter of state criminal law to other surgical situations, is unduly restrictive of the patient's rights, which are already safeguarded by her personal physician. Pp. 15-17.

(c) Required acquiescence by two co-practitioners also has no rational connection with a patient's needs and unduly infringes on her physician's right to practise. Pp. 17-19.

5. The Georgia residence requirement violates the Privileges and Immunities Clause by denying protection to persons who enter Georgia for medical services there. Pp. 19-20.

6. Appellants' equal protection argument centring on the three procedural conditions in § 26-1202 (b), invalidated on other grounds, is without merit. P. 20.

7. No ruling is made on the question of injunctive relief. Cf. *Roe* v. *Wade, supra.* P. 20.

319 F. Supp. 1048, modified and affirmed.

Blackmun, J., delivered the opinion of the Court, in which Burger, C. J., and Douglas, Brennan, Stewart, Marshall, and Powell, J-J., joined. Burger, C. J., and Douglas, J., filed concurring opinions. White, J., filed a dissenting opinion, in which Rehnquist, J., joined. Rehnquist, J., filed a dissenting opinion.

2

The following opinion and summary of the US Supreme Court decisions have been prepared by the legal counsel of Planned Parenthood of New York City Inc.[3] This explains in simple and non-legal language the implications of the Supreme Court decisions for all the states of the Union.

> In the 'Texas' case, the Court held that the right of privacy 'is broad enough to encompass a woman's decision whether or not to terminate her pregnancy'. The Court also said that the right is not absolute and is subject to some limitations, which the Court spelled out and which are summarized below.
>
> The Court held that the word 'person' as used in the Fourteenth Amendment does not include the unborn. It ruled that the foetus has no constitutional rights.
>
> Beyond this, the essence of the 'Texas' case is that criminal abortion statutes such as the Texas statute which permit abortion only to save the mother's life violate the right of privacy protected by the Due Process Clause of the Fourteenth Amendment.
>
> The Court said that up to approximately the end of the first trimester, the state can have no voice in the decision to have an abortion and that the performance of the abortion must be left to the medical judgement of the woman's physician.
>
> Following the first trimester of pregnancy, the state – in promoting its interest in the health of the mother – may in the second trimester, if it chooses, regulate the abortion procedure in ways that are reasonably

[3] Courtesy of Attorney Harriet F. Pilpel *et al.* of Greenbaum, Wolf & Ernst and Planned Parenthood of New York City, Inc.

related to maternal health but may not limit the grounds for abortion. The Court held that in the second trimester the state has a legitimate interest in seeing to it that abortions are performed under circumstances that ensure maximum safety for the patient. This interest includes such factors as the performing physician and his staff, the abortion facility itself, the availability of after-care, and adequate provision for any emergency or complication that might arise.

In the third trimester, after the foetus becomes capable of 'meaningful' life outside the mother's womb, a state, in promoting its interest in the 'potentiality of human life', *may* regulate or even forbid abortion except when it is necessary to preserve the life or health of the mother. (It seems clear that health includes mental health.)

With reference to all three trimesters, the state *may* define the word 'physician' to mean only a physician currently licensed by the state and may forbid abortions from being performed by any other person.

The Georgia law permitted abortion to protect the life or health of the woman, or where the foetus was likely to be born with a serious defect, or where the pregnancy resulted from rape. These limitations are invalid for the first and second trimesters under the principles enunciated by the Court in the Texas case. In the 'Georgia' case, the Court also struck down the following requirements: that abortions be performed in a hospital accredited by the Joint Commission on Accreditation of Hospitals; that abortions be approved by a hospital committee; that two additional physicians confirm a woman's need to have an abortion; that abortions be restricted to residents of the state. The Court held that all of these requirements were invalid at any time during pregnancy.

The Court also said that after the first trimester, upon a proper showing of the need therefore to protect maternal health, a state may require that abortions be performed in a licensed hospital.

What the Decisions Mean to Other States

The Texas decision invalidates all state laws which prohibit abortions except for those necessary to preserve the life of the mother. Statutes of this type were on the books in thirty states besides Texas (although in some of these states lower courts had already declared some of them unconstitutional). The laws in effect in these states which apply generally to medical practice would in any event remain in effect with respect to abortion.

Thirteen states had laws patterned after Georgia's. The parts of those laws which limited the grounds for abortion in the first two trimesters are now invalid. Some other provisions of these statutes are also inconsistent with the Supreme Court's ruling.

Alabama and the District of Columbia had laws generally permitting abortion for reasons of the life and health of the woman. These statutes also are inconsistent with the Supreme Court's decisions regarding at least first trimester abortions, and may be inconsistent with the Supreme Court decisions in other respects as well.

The statutes in the four so-called repeal states (Alaska, Hawaii, New York and Washington) are more consistent with the Supreme Court's decisions, but in some respects they, too, do not comply with the decisions.

States may enact new laws regulating abortion, but such laws must be consistent with these decisions of the Supreme Court.

What the Decisions Mean to New York State

The New York law comes closest to the specifications of the decisions. However, the New York law is also inconsistent with the decisions in that New York permits abortion after twenty-four weeks of pregnancy only to preserve the woman's life, whereas the Court ruled that abortions must be permitted to preserve the woman's life or *health* even after viability.

With regard to New York City's health code regulations specifically relating to abortion, we agree with New York City Health Services Administrator Gordon Chase that in their present form these appear to be unconstitutional with respect to the first trimester. It is unclear to what extent they are valid with respect to the second and third trimesters.

A few key questions may be raised and answered:

1. When do the Supreme Court decisions go into effect?

Based on generally applicable principles of law and the Supreme Court's statements in both cases, we believe that the decisions became effective when they were handed down, namely, on January 22, 1973. In our opinion, it is not necessary for statutes which are unconstitutional to be repealed; the Supreme Court decisions supersede state laws inconsistent with them.

2. What abortion regulations are now permitted?

In the first trimester of pregnancy, the only valid regulation of abortion as such is one proscribing the performance of an abortion by anyone except a licensed physician.

In the second trimester, only such regulations of abortion as are 'reasonably related to maternal health' and are not discriminatory in singling out the abortion procedure are permissible. The grounds for abortion may not be limited. Examples given by the Court of permissible regulations are 'requirements as to the qualifications of the person who is to perform the abortion; as to the licensure of that person; as to the facility in which the procedure is to be performed, that is, whether it must be a hospital or may be a clinic or some other place of less-than-hospital status; as to the licensing of the facility; and the like'.

In the third trimester, laws forbidding abortion for the purpose of promoting the state's 'interest in the potentiality of human life' are valid unless abortion is necessary, in appropriate medical judgement, for the preservation of the life or health of the mother. Health includes 'mental health'. Also permissible in the third trimester are the same type of

APPENDIXES

regulations 'reasonably related to the maternal health' which are allowed in the second trimester.

3. How do the Supreme Court decisions affect endometrial aspiration?

Since endometrial aspiration is by definition possible only in the early part of the first trimester, if it is an abortion, it is subject to the same rules as other first trimester abortions.

4. Can licensed physicians now legally perform abortions in the first trimester on any ground?

Yes.

5. In the light of the Supreme Court rulings, is it necessary for a state to have an abortion law?

No. Many people believe that abortion is like any other medical procedure and should be governed by the same laws as apply to medical practice generally.

6. What happens to pending proceedings in lower courts in the light of the Supreme Court rulings?

With reference to criminal proceedings in which the time to appeal has not expired, a simple motion to dismiss the prosecution on the basis of the Supreme Court decisions should be sufficient. Test cases will no doubt be disposed of summarily. All state and federal courts are, of course, bound by the decisions of the United States Supreme Court.

Glossary

ABORTIFACIENT: producing abortion; an agent producing abortion.

ABORTION: the delivery of an embryo or foetus to the stage of viability of about 20 weeks of gestation when the foetus normally weighs less than 400 grams. Abortion is different from premature birth. Abortion may be spontaneous or induced.

    ACCIDENTAL ABORTION: caused by a blow, fall or any other accidental injury.

    AFEBRILE ABORTION: resulting from pregnancy in tubal ampulla or saccular anatomic swelling or pouch.

    COMPLETE ABORTION: one in which all the products of conception have been expelled entirely from the uterus and identified.

    CRIMINAL ABORTION: termination of pregnancy without any medical, legal or other justification; meaning varies according to the laws in force in a country.

    EARLY ABORTION: expulsion from the uterus of an embryo weighing less than 400 grams, measuring less than 28 cm and of less than 22 weeks of gestation.

    HABITUAL ABORTION: a condition in which a woman has had three or more consecutive spontaneous abortions.

    IMMINENT ABORTION: an incipient or threatened abortion, in which there is profuse vaginal bleeding, a softened and dilated cervix and cramps similar to labour pains.

    INCOMPLETE ABORTION: in which part of the product of conception has been passed but part (usually the placenta) remains in the uterus.

    INDUCED ABORTION: an abortion brought about intentionally by drugs or surgery or other mechanical means.

    INEVITABLE ABORTION: brought about by the rupture of the membranes in the presence of cervical dilation; abortion in progress.

    INFECTIOUS ABORTION: an abortion resulting from an infectious disease.

    JUSTIFIABLE ABORTION: a therapeutic abortion done to save the life of the mother.

    MISSED ABORTION: one in which the foetus is dead *in utero* but the product of conception retained *in utero* for at least 2 months.

    NATURAL ABORTION: one that has not been artificially induced.

    SEPTIC ABORTION: an abortion in which the tissue of the uterus is infected; complicated by fever, endometritis and parametritis.

    SPONTANEOUS ABORTION: natural abortion.

    THERAPEUTIC ABORTION: an abortion induced because of the mother's poor health.

    THREATENED ABORTION: painful cramps and slight discharge of blood which may or may not be followed by the expulsion of the foetus during the first 20 weeks of pregnancy.

    TUBAL ABORTION: termination of a tubal pregnancy (ectopic) through the rupture of the fallopian tube.

GLOSSARY

ACHARYA: teacher; preceptor; commentator.
AHIMSA: literally non-violence.
AMENORRHEA: absence of abnormal cessation of the menses.
AMNIOTIC FLUID: the serous fluid in the closed thin membrane sac (called the amnion) in which the embryo is immersed and which protects it against mechanical injury.
ATMAN: soul; the conscious self; life principle.
AYURVEDA: ancient Hindu indigenous system of medicine.
AZL (or AZAL or AL-AZH): the term for *coitus interruptus* practised by early Arabs.
BLASTOCYST: an early stage in the development of the embryo.
BRUNA-HATYA (foetus murder): literally feticide; abortion.
CALOTROPIC GIGANTEA: a plant in tropical India, a twig of which is used for induced abortion.
D AND C (DILATATION AND CURETTAGE): see p. 56 for a brief description of the surgical procedure.
DOSHA: humour theory of temperament.
-ECTOMY: suffix meaning the removal of, as in the terms vasectomy and tubectomy.
FATWA: Muslim ecclesiastical pronouncement.
FIQH: Islamic jurisprudence.
MEIOSIS: special cell division that occurs during the development of gametes, lessening the number of chromosomes in the cell.
MUFTI: Muslim ecclesiastical head.
NEONATAL DEATH: the death of an infant below the age of one month.
ONANISM: *coitus interruptus*; withdrawal before the completion of the sexual act to prevent insemination; after Onan, son of Judah who practised it.
PANCHAYAT: village council consisting of five elders elected by the people; can be expanded to a larger democratically elected council.
PANCHAYATI RAJ: administration through Panchayat, i.e. people.
PRAJAPATI (*praja-pati*, creation's king): title of early Vedic gods.
PREMATURE BIRTH: the birth of an infant after the stage of viability of about 20 weeks but before full term of 9 months.
PUSHAN: deity as represented by the sun.
RUBELLA: German measles, an acute exanthematous disease resembling in several respects both measles and scarlet fever. The exposure of a pregnant woman during the first 3 months to rubella creates a 10 to 50 per cent probability that the infant, if born, may suffer from heart disease, blindness, mental retardation, or face early death.
SHARIAT: Islamic law.
SIDDHA: ancient South Indian Hindu system of medicine. Believed to be older than Ayurveda.
STILL BIRTH: a foetal death occurring after 28 weeks of pregnancy.
SUNNAH: Islamic tradition.
TUBECTOMY: salpingectomy; removal of all or part of the Fallopian tube; a method of female sterilization.

ULEMA: Muslim ecclesiastical head; a scholar or divine trained in Muslim theology and law, and recognized as an authority in these fields.

UNANI: Indian Muslim system of medicine; was brought into India by the invading Mughals; can be traced back to the Greeks.

VACUUM ASPIRATOR: see p. 57 for a brief description.

VASECTOMY: excision of a segment of the vas deferens in which the spermatozoa are conveyed; a method of male sterilization.

VIABLE FOETUS: a foetus whose period of gestation has lasted sufficiently long (about 28 weeks) to permit extra-uterine life.

ZYGOTE: the fertilized ovum; the individual produced by the fusion of two cells.

Select Bibliography

Abortion Act, 1967 (London, HMSO, 1967).
Anand, D., 'Clinico-Epidemiological Study of Abortions', *Indian Journal of Public Health*, (January 1965).
Anshen, Ruth Nanda (ed.), *The Family: Its Function and Destiny* (New York, Harpers, 1949).
Aptekar, Herbert, *Infanticide, Contraception and Abortion in Savage Society* (New York, Godwin, 1931).
Baer, Gabriel, *Population and Society in the Arab East* (New York, Praeger, 1964).
Banerjee, D. and Mukherjee, S. P., 'Some Quantitative Aspects of Labour and Abortion in India', *Calcutta Medical Journal* (May and September 1962).
Basham, A. L., *The Wonder that was India* (New York, Grove Press, 1959).
Bates, Jerome E. and Zawadzki, Edward S., *Criminal Abortion* (Springfield, Illinois, Charles C. Thomas, 1964).
Beck, Dorothy Faho, 'The Changing Muslim Family of the Middle East', *Marriage and Family Living* (November 1957).
Beck, Mildred B. *et al.*, 'Abortion: A National Public and Mental Health Problem – Past, Present and Proposed Research', *American Journal of Public Health* (December 1969).
Bende, Asha, *Abortion Rates Among the Currently Married Women in Greater Bombay* (Bombay, Demographic Training and Research Centre, 1967); mimeographed paper.
Biswas, Nilima, 'The Trend of Fertility and Vital Loss of Pregnancy in an Urban Community', *Journal of the Indian Medical Association* (1 July 1968).
Bose, Ashish, Desai, P. B., and Jain, S. P., *Studies in Demography*, essays presented in honour of S. Chandrasekhar (London, Allen & Unwin, 1970; Chapel Hill, University of North Carolina Press, 1971).
Bose, Sudhir, 'Abortion: A Clinical Review of 1217 Cases', *Journal of Obstetrics and Gynaecology of India* (September 1959).
Boulding, Kenneth E., *The Meaning of the Twentieth Century: The Great Transition* (New York, Harper & Row, 1965).
Bracket, J. W. and Depaw, J. W., *Population Policy and Demographic Trends in the Soviet Union* (Washington, D.C., U.S. Government Printing Office, 1966).
Breznik, D., 'Fertility of the Yugoslav Population', in E. Szabady *et al.* (eds), *World Views of Population Problems* (Budapest, Akademiai Kiado, 1968).
Browne, Stella *et al.*, *Abortion* (London, Allen & Unwin, 1935).
Bulgaria: laws, statutes, etc. 'Interruption of Pregnancy', *International Digest of Health Legislation* (1968:19).
Calderone, Mary S. (ed.), *Abortion in the United States* (New York, Hoeber-Harper, 1958).
Callahan, Daniel, *Abortion: Law, Choice and Morality* (New York, Macmillan, 1970).

Campbell, J., 'Abortion in Russia', *The Eugenics Review* (1965:57).
Castiglioni, Arturo, *A History of Medicine*, trans. from Italian, ed. E. B. Krumbhaar (New York, 1941).
Census of India, 1951, Report, vol. 1, part 1A (New Delhi, Government of India Press, 1953).
Census of India, 1951, Estimation of Births and Deaths in India During 1941–50 (New Delhi, Government of India Press, 1954).
Census of India, 1961, Paper No. 1 of 1962 (New Delhi, Government of India Press, 1962).
Census of India, 1961, vol. 1, part 1A, *Levels of Regional Development in India*, Part 1 of the General Report on India (New Delhi, Government of India Press, 1964).
Census of India, 1971, Paper No. 1 of 1971 (New Delhi, Government of India Press, 1972).
Chandrasekhar, S., 'Prospect of Planned Parenthood in India', *Pacific Affairs* (December 1953).
——'Population Growth, Socio-Economic Development and Living Standards', *International Labour Review* (July 1954).
——'The Family in India', *Marriage and Family Living* (November 1954).
——*Hungry People and Empty Lands*, 3rd edn., (London, Allen & Unwin; New York, Macmillan, 1954).
——'Infant Mortality in India', *Proceedings of the World Population Conference, Rome, 1954* (New York, United Nations, 1955).
——'Some Observations on Infant Mortality in India', *The Eugenics Review* (January 1955).
——'Cultural Barriers to Family Planning in Underdeveloped Countries', *The Rationalist Annual* (London, December 1955).
——'Family Planning in Rural India', *Antioch Review* (Spring 1959).
——'A Note on Demographic Statistics in India', *Population Review* (January 1960).
——*Population and Planned Parenthood in India*, with forewords by Jawaharlal Nehru and Sir Julian Huxley, 2nd edn. (London, Allen & Unwin; New York, Macmillan, 1961).
——'A Billion Indians by AD 2000', *The New York Times Magazine*, (4 April 1965).
——'The Role of Abortion in Population Control', *The Statesman* (New Delhi, 9 June 1966).
——'Should we Legalize Abortion in India?', *Population Review* (July 1966).
——'Should Abortion be Legalized in India?', *The Illustrated Weekly of India* (Bombay, 16 October 1966).
——'Asia's Population Problems', in Guy Wint (ed.), *Asia: A Handbook* (London, Anthony Bond; New York, Praeger, 1966).
——'Infant Mortality in Madras City', *Proceedings of the World Population Conference, Belgrade, 1965* (New York, United Nations, 1966).
—— (ed.), *Asia's Population Problems* (London, Allen & Unwin; New York, Praeger, 1967).

SELECT BIBLIOGRAPHY

──────'Population Control Successful in India', *Journal of the American Medical Association* (3 June 1968).
──────'India's Population Policy', the (Manchester) *Guardian* (15 August 1968).
──────'How India is Tackling her Population Problem', *Foreign Affairs* (October 1968).
──────'Abortion: A Socio-Medical Problem', *The Hindu Sunday Magazine* (8 June 1969).
──────'A Liberal Policy on Abortion', *The Hindu Sunday Magazine* (15 June 1969).
──────*India's Population: Fact, Problem and Policy*, 2nd edn. (Meerut, Meenakshi Prakashan, 1970).
──────'Abortion in India', in Robert E. Hall (ed.), *Abortion in a Changing World* (New York, Columbia University Press, 1970).
──────'India: Two must do', *Ecology Today* (September 1971).
──────*Infant Mortality, Population Growth and Family Planning in India* (London, Allen & Unwin; Chapel Hill, University of North Carolina Press, 1972).
Charaka, *Charaka Samhita*, 3rd edn. (Poona, Nirnaya Sagar Press, 1941).
Charaka Samhita (Varanasi, Motilal Banarsidas, 1948).
Chatterjee, Saral K. (ed.), *Legalization of Abortion* (Madras, Christian Literature Society, 1971).
Chaudhuri, Nirad C., 'Legalized Abortion', *NOW* (25 February 1966).
Chester, Eustace, *Society and Abortion* (London, Abortion Law Reform Association, 1949).
The Church (of England) Assembly Board for Social Responsibility, *Abortion: An Ethical Discussion* (London, 1965).
Compston, Nigel D. (ed.), *The Cost of Life: Proceedings of the Royal Society of Medicine* (London, 1967).
Cooke, Robert E., Hellegers, Andre E., Hoyt, Robert G., and Richardson, Herbert W., *The Terrible Choice: The Abortion Dilemma* (New York, Bantam Books, 1968).
Corner, George W., *Ourselves Unborn: An Embryologist's Essay on Man* (New Haven, Yale University Press, 1948).
Dandekar, Kumidini, *Demographic Survey of Six Rural Communities* (Poona, Gokhale Institute of Politics and Economics, 1959).
Danielou, Alain, *Hindu Polytheism* (New York, Pantheon Books, 1964).
David, Henry P., *Family Planning and Abortion in the Socialist Countries of Central and Eastern Europe: A Compendium of Observation and Readings* (New York, the Population Council, 1970).
David, J. C., 'Liberalization of Abortion as a Measure to Control Population', *Journal of the Christian Medical Association* (Nagpur, August 1969).
Devereux, George, *A Study of Abortion in Primitive Societies* (New York, Julian Press, 1955).
Diczfalusy, Egon and Borrell, Ulf (eds.), *Control of Human Fertility*, Nobel Symposium 15 (New York, Wiley Interscience Division, 1971).
Djerassi, Carl, 'Fertility Control Through Abortion: An Assessment of the Period 1950–80', *Bulletin of the Atomic Scientists* (January 1972).

Durant, Will, *The Story of Philosophy* (New York, Simon & Schuster, 1961).
Dvorak, Z. *et al.*, 'The Termination of Pregnancy by Vacuum Aspiration', *The Lancet* (11 November 1967).
Ebling, F. J. (ed.), *Biology and Ethics* (London and New York, Academic Press, 1969).
Ellis, Havelock, *Studies in the Psychology of Sex* (New York, Random House, 1936).
Family Planning. Training and Research Centre, Bombay: 'Random Sample of Incidence of Abortion from 1,000 Family Case Card Histories', *Five Year Report, 1957–62* (Bombay, Family Planning. Training and Research Centre, 1962).
Ferris, Paul, *The Nameless: Abortion in Britain Today* (London, Hutchinson, 1966).
Fletcher, Joseph, *Morals and Medicine* (Princeton, Princeton University Press, 1954).
Francis, O., 'An Analysis of 1,150 Cases of Abortions from the Government R.S.M. Lying-In Hospital, Madras', *Journal of Obstetrics and Gynaecology of India* (September 1959).
Fredericksen, H., and Brackett, J. W., 'Demographic Effects of Abortion', *Public Health Reports* (1968, 83 (12)).
Gandhi, M. K., *Birth Control: The Right Way and the Wrong Way* (Ahmedabad, Navajivan, 1959).
Gebhard, Paul *et al.*, *Pregnancy, Birth and Abortion* (New York, Hoeber-Harper, 1958).
Geiger, H. K., *The Family in Soviet Russia* (Cambridge, Harvard University Press, 1968).
Geijerstam, Gunnar K. A., *An Annotated Bibliography of Induced Abortion* (Ann Arbor, University of Michigan, 1969).
Gold, Edwin M. *et al.*, *Therapeutic Abortions in New York City: A Twenty Year Review* (New York City, Department of Health, Bureau of Records and Statistics, 1963).
Goyal, R. P., *A Study of Abortion Among Railway Workers in Delhi* (Delhi, Demographic Research Centre, Institute of Economic Growth, no date); mimeographed paper.
Granfield, David, *The Abortion Decision* (Garden City, New York, Doubleday, 1969).
Grisez, Germain, *Abortion: The Myths, the Realities and the Arguments* (New York, Corpus Books, 1970).
Gutmacher, Alan F. (ed.), *The Case for Legalized Abortion Now* (Berkeley, California, Diablo Press, 1967).
Hague, Zohrul, 'Family Planning and Islam', *The Islamic Review* (July–August 1958).
Hall, Robert E., (ed.), *Abortion in a Changing World*, 2 vols (New York, Columbia University Press, 1970).
Haneman, E., and the editors of *Life*, *Birth Control* (New York, Time International, 1967).
Hardin, Garrett, *Abortion and Human Dignity*, public lecture given at the University of California, Berkeley (1964).

SELECT BIBLIOGRAPHY

———'The History and Future of Birth Control', *Perspectives in Biology and Medicine*, vol. 10, no. 1 (Autumn 1966).

———'Semantic Aspect of Abortion', *ETC: A Review of General Semantics* (September 1967).

———'Birth Control – the Prospects', *Medicine Today* (October 1967).

———'Blueprints, DNA and Abortion: Scientific and Ethical Analysis', *Medical Opinion and Review* (September 1967).

———*Population, Evolution and Birth Control: A Collage of Controversial Readings*, 2nd edn. (San Francisco, W. H. Freeman, 1970).

———'Abortion or Compulsory Pregnancy?', *Journal of Marriage and Family*, vol. 30, no. 2 (1968).

———'The Tragedy of the Commons', *Science* (13 December 1968).

Harrington, Michael, *Poverty, Family Planning and the Great Society* (New York, Planned Parenthood Federation, 1966).

Haughton, G. C. (ed.), *Manava Dharma-Sastra* (translation) (London, Cox & Baylis, 1825).

Heer, D. M., 'Abortion, Contraception and Population Policy in the Soviet Union', *Demography* (1965:2).

Himes, Norman E., *Medical History of Contraception* (New York, Schocken Books, 1970).

Hindell, Keith and Simms, Madeleine, 'How the Abortion Lobby Worked', *The Political Quarterly* (July–September 1968).

Hopkins, Edward (ed.), Burnell, Arthur C. (translation), *Ordinances of Manu* (London, Kegan Paul, 1891).

Hren, M., Herak-Szabo, J., and Mojic, A., 'Abortion in Yugoslavia', *Excerpta Medica* (1964).

Institute of Rural Health and Family Planning, Gandhigram: 'A Report on the Incidence of Abortion as Studied from the Data Compiled at the Kasturba Maternity Hospital, Gandhigram', *Quarterly Bulletin of Pilot Health Project* (Gandhigram, October 1961).

———'A Report on the Incidence of Abortion in a Weaver Community in the Project Area', *Quarterly Bulletin of Pilot Health Project* (Gandhigram, July 1963).

Israel, Sarah, *Some Observations on Abortion* (Bombay, Family Planning Training and Research Centre, 1967); mimeographed paper.

Jacobi, Hermann, *The Gaina Sutras: The Sacred Books of the East* (translation), vol. 22 (Oxford, Clarendon Press, 1884).

Jain, S. P., 'Fertility Trends in Greater Bombay', a paper presented at the Conference of the International Union for the Scientific Study of Population, Sydney, Australia (August 1967).

Jakobovits, Immanuel, *Jewish Medical Ethics* (New York, Philosophical Library, 1959).

Jenkins, Alice, *Law for the Rich* (London, Gollancz, 1961).

Khan, Akter Hameed, *Islamic Opinions on Contraception* (Dacca, 1963).

Kimura, M., 'A Review of Induced Abortion Surveys in Japan', *International Population Conference* (New York, 1961).

Klinger, A., 'Demographic Effects of Abortion Legislation in Some

European Socialist Countries', *Proceedings of the World Population Conference, Belgrade*, vol. 2 (New York, United Nations, 1967).

Klobroria, V., 'Legal Abortion in Czechoslovakia', *Journal of the American Medical Association* (1966, 196:371).

Koya, Y., 'A Study of Induced Abortion in Japan', *Milbank Memorial Fund Quarterly* (July, 1954).

Kucera, M., 'The Abortion Rate in Czechoslovakia', *Czechoslovak Population Problems* (Prague, 1969).

Labbry, Daniel H. et al., *Life or Death: Ethics and Options* (Seattle, University of Washington Press, 1968).

Lader, Lawrence, *Abortion* (New York, Bobbs-Merrill, 1966).

——'The Scandal of Abortion Laws', *The New York Times Magazine* (25 April 1965).

Lee, Nancy Howell, *The Search for an Abortionist* (Chicago, University of Chicago Press, 1969).

Levy, Reuben, *The Social Structure of Islam* (London, Cambridge University Press, 1957).

Lindahl, J., *Somatic Complications Following Legal Abortion* (Stockholm, Svenska Bokforleget, 1959).

Lowe, David, *Abortion and the Law* (New York, Pocket Books, 1966).

Manson, Margaret M. et al., 'Rubella and Other Virus Infections during Pregnancy', *Ministry of Health Reports on Public Health and Medical Subjects* (London, HMSO, 1960).

Mehlan, K. H., *The Effects of Legalization of Abortion in Eastern Europe*, no. 72 (Amsterdam, Medica Foundation, 1964).

——'Legal Abortion in Romania', *Journal of Sex Research* (1965:1).

Mukerjee, S., and Biswas, S., 'Previous Abortions and their Relationship to Current Terminations and Socio-Economic Status Based on Hospital Data', *The Journal of Obstetrics and Gynaecology of India* (September 1959).

Muller, Max (ed.), *Sacred Books of the East* (Oxford, Clarendon Press, 1879).

Muramatsu, Minoru, 'Effect of Induced Abortion on Reduction of Births in Japan', *Milbank Memorial Fund Quarterly* (April 1960).

Muslim Views on Family Planning (Mysore, State Family Planning Bureau, 1969).

National Committee on Maternal Health: *The Abortion Problem* (Baltimore, Williams & Wilkins, 1944).

Needham, Joseph, *A History of Embryology* (Cambridge, Cambridge University Press, 1959).

Noonan, J. T., *Contraception: A History of its Treatment by the Catholic Theologians and Canonists* (Cambridge, Harvard University Press, 1966).

——*The Morality of Abortion* (Cambridge, Harvard University Press, 1970).

Pakter, Jean and Nelson, Frieda, 'Abortion in New York City: The First Nine Months', *Family Planning Perspectives* (vol. 3, no. 3, New York, July 1971).

Parliament of India, Rajya Sabha: *Joint Committee on the Medical Termina-*

tion of Pregnancy Bill, 1969 Evidence, vols 1 and 2 (New Delhi, Rajya Sabha Secretariat, November 1970).
────*The Medical Termination of Pregnancy Bill 1969: Report of the Joint Committee* (New Delhi, Rajya Sabha Secretariat, November 1970).
Petersen, William, *Population*, 2nd edn. (New York, Macmillan, 1969).
Pilpel, Harriet F., 'The Right of Abortion', *Atlantic Monthly* (June 1969).
Pilpel, Harriet F. and Norwick, Kenneth P., *When Should Abortion be Legal* (New York) Public Affairs Pamphlet, 1970).
Population and the American Future: The Report of the Commission on Population Growth and the American Future (New York, The American Library, 1972).
Potter, R. G., Jr, 'Birth Intervals: Structure and Change', *Population Studies* (November 1963).
Potter, R. G. *et al.*, 'Foetal Wastage in Eleven Punjab Villages', *Human Biology* (September 1965).
Potts, Malcolm, 'Legal Abortion in Eastern Europe', *The Eugenics Review* (December 1967).
Radhakrishnan, S., *The Hindu View of Life* (London, Allen & Unwin, 1951).
────*The Principal Upanishads* (London, Allen & Unwin, 1953).
Rao, B. K., 'Induced Abortions – a Critical Survey', *Medical Digest*, 33: 256 (1965).
Rao, Hari P., *Indian Penal Code* (Act XLV of 1860 as amended to end of 1925) (Madras, Law Publishing House, 1965).
Report of the Committee to Study the Question of the Legalization of Abortion (New Delhi, Ministry of Health and Family Planning, 1966).
Roemar, Ruth, 'Abortion Law: The Approaches of Different Nations', *American Journal of Public Health* (November 1967).
Rosen, Harold, *Therapeutic Abortion* (New York, Julian Press, 1954).
────(ed.), *Abortion in America* (Boston, Beacon Press, 1967).
Rossi, Alice S., 'Social Change and Abortion Law Reform', *Dissent* (July–August 1969).
────'Abortion Laws and their Victims', *Trans-Action* (September–October 1966).
Schieffelin, Olivia (ed.), *Muslim Attitudes toward Family Planning* (New York, the Population Council, 1967).
Schur, Edwin M., *Crimes Without Victims* (Englewood Cliffs, New Jersey, Prentice Hall, 1965).
Schwartz, Herman, 'A Survey of Abortion Law Reform', *Humanist* (July–August 1967).
Sengupta, B., 'Liberalization of Abortion as a Population Control Measure', *Indian Journal of Public Health*, 9:69 (1965).
Shaw, Russell, *Abortion on Trial* (Dayton, Ohio, George A. Pflaum, 1968).
Simms, Madeleine, 'Abortion Law Reform', *Humanist* (November 1964).
Singer, Charles, *A Short History of Anatomy from the Greeks to Harvey* (New York, Dover, 1957).
Smith, David T. (ed.), *Abortion and the Law* (Cleveland, Case Western Reserve University Press, 1968).

Storer, Horatio R., *Criminal Abortion in America* (Philadelphia, Lippincott, 1966).
Susruta, *Susruta Samhita* (with a commentary by Dalhana) (Bombay, Nirnaya Sagar Press, 1915).
Szabady, E., 'Family Planning Trends: The Hungarian Study', *Demografia* (1968:11).
Szabady, E. *et al.*, (eds.), *World Views of Population Problems* (Budapest, Akademiai Kiado, 1966).
Taussig, Frederick J., *Abortion: Spontaneous and Induced* (St Louis: Mosby Co., 1936).
The Abortion Act, 1967, proceedings of a symposium held by the Medical Protection Society, London, 1969 (London, Pitman Medical Publishing Co., 1969).
The Abortion Problem, proceedings of a conference under the auspices of the National Committee on Maternal Health (Baltimore, Williams & Wilkins, 1944).
Thomlinson, R., *Population Dynamics* (New York, Random House, 1965).
Thurtle, Dorothy, *Abortion: Right or Wrong* (London, Watts, 1940).
Tien, Yuan H., 'Induced Abortion and Population Control in Mainland China', *Marriage and Family Living* (February 1963).
Tietze, C., 'The Demographic Significance of Legal Abortion in Eastern Europe', *Demography* (1964:1).
───'Abortion in Europe', *American Journal of Public Health* (November 1967).
United Kingdom, Office of Population Censuses and Surveys: *The Registrar General's Statistical Review of England and Wales for the Year 1968. Supplement on Abortion* (London, HMSO, 1970).
Urlanis, B. T., 'Dynamics of the Birthrate in the U.S.S.R. and Factors Contributing to it', *Proceedings of the World Population Conference, Belgrade*, vol. 2 (New York, United Nations, 1967).
───'The Birthrate in the U.S.S.R. after the Second World War', paper presented at the Conference of the International Union for the Scientific Study of Population (London 1969).
Vincent, Clark E., *Unmarried Mothers* (Glencoe, Illinois, Free Press, 1961).
Vojta, M., 'A Critical View of Vacuum Aspiration: A New Method for the Termination of Pregnancy', *Obstetrics and Gynaecology* (July 1967).
Vostrikova, A. M., 'Examination of Fertility, Marriages and Family in the USSR', in E. Szabady (ed.) *Studies on Fertility and Social Mobility* (Budapest, Akademiai Kiado, 1964).
Westoff, Charles F. *et al.*, 'The Structure of Attitudes Toward Abortion', *Milbank Memorial Fund Quarterly* (January 1969).
Whitney, W. D., *The Atharva Veda Samhita* (translation) (Varanasi, Motilal Banarsidas, 1962).
Who Shall Live? Man's Control over Birth and Death, Report prepared for the American Friends Service Committee (New York, Hill & Wang, 1970).

SELECT BIBLIOGRAPHY

Williams, Glanville, *The Sanctity of Life and the Criminal Law* (New York, Knopf, 1957).

Wimperis, Virginia, *The Unmarried Mother and her Child* (London, Allen & Unwin, 1960).

World Health Organization: *Abortion Laws: A Survey of Current World Legislation* (Geneva, 1971).

Yugoslavia: *General Law on the Interruption of Pregnancy*, Government Paper no. 20 (Belgrade, 1969).

Zimmer, Heinrich, *Myths and Symbols in Indian Art and Civilization* (New York, Pantheon, 1946).

———*Hindu Medicine* (Baltimore, Johns Hopkins Press, 1948).

Index of Names

Abbas, Ibn 46
Adams, Dr 30
Amberly, Lord 153
Amulree, Lord 53
Anand, D. 64
Anshen, Ruth Nanda 46
Aquinas, St Thomas 26
Aristotle 24–5, 51
Augustine, St 25, 26

Bende, Asha 63
Benedict XV, Pope 27
Blackmun, Justice 162, 164
Bloomfield, M. 41
Birkett, Lord 51
Biswas, S. 64
Bourne, Alec 52, 53
Brennan, Justice 162, 164
Buhler, George 42
Burger, W. 162, 164

Castiglioni, Arturo 43
Chandrasekhar, Sripati 15, 38, 48, 68 87, 113, 146, 149, 150, 151, 156, 157
Charaka 23, 42, 43
Chase, Gordon 166
Corner, George W. 29

Dandekar, K. 61
Danielou, Alain 41
Danz, Jessie 13
Danz, John 11, 13
David, Henry P. 55
David, J. C. 151
Devereaux, George 22
Digby, Simon Wingfield 53
Djerassi, Carl 58, 65
Douglas, Justice 162, 164
Duce, Il see Mussolini
Durant, Will 24, 25

Ebling, F. J. 31

Franco, General 34

Gandhi, Mohandas Karamchand 33, 45
Gandhi, Mrs Indira 75

George III 50
Gertig, Dr 30
Goyal, R. P. 64
Grisez, Germain 41

Hall, Robert E. 29, 48, 54
Haneman, E. 59
Hardin, Garett 11, 15, 29, 31
Harper, P. A. 111
Heer, D. M. 112
Himes, Norman E. 22
Hotey, K. 115

Israel, Sarah 63

Jaffery, Arthur 46

Krumbhar, E. B. 43

Lader, Lawrence 52
Lenin 49
Lolimbaraj, Acharya 45

McCarthy, Joseph L. 11
McKerron, Jane 160
Macnaughten, Mr Justice 52
Madhavikara 42
Mahatma, see Gandhi, M. K.
Mahopatra, P. S. 142
Manu 42
Marshall, Justice 162, 164
Mehlan, K. H. 54
Mehta, Pushpa 157
Menaka 157
Menon, Panampalli Govinda 88
Misra, Bava 42
Mohammed, Prophet 46
Mufti, Grand (of Egypt) 47
Mukherjee, S. 64
Muller, F. Max 41–2
Muramatsu, Minoru 111, 112
Mussolini 34

Nagarjuna 42
Narain, Raj 157
Nazer, Isam R. 48
Nixon, Richard M. 54
Noonan, Jr, John T. 26

Odegaard, Charles E. 11

Paranjpye, Shakuntala 156
Paul VI, Pope 27, 151
Peter, St 34
Petersen, William 55
Petrovsky, Boris 57
Pilpel, Harriet F. 164
Pius XII, Pope 27
Plato 24
Pleasants, Julian 37
Potter, R. G. 60, 112
Potts, Malcolm 31
Powell, Justice 162, 164
Prajapati 41
Pushan 41

Queen Victoria 51

Radharishnan, S. 32, 34, 45
Ramanuja Acharya 40
Reeves, Joseph 53
Rehnquist, Justice 162, 164
Riddell, Lord 31
Roberts, Thomas D. 37
Robinson, Kenneth 53
Rock, Dr 30
Rockefeller, John III 53
Russell, Bertrand 153

Sankara Acharya 40
Sayeed, Abu 47
Schweitzer, Albert 35
Shah, Shantilal 83, 128, 148, 152, 157
Shakuntala 157
Shaw, George Bernard 35
Shivapari, S. 98–9
Short, Renee 53
Silkin, Lord 53
Snow, Edgar 50
Ssu-Mo, Sun 24
Stewart, Justice 162, 164
Susruta 42–3
Szabady, Egon 114–15

Tendulkar, D. G. 33
Thomlinson, R. 55

Vaghbata I 42
Vaghbata II 42
Vatsyayana 26
Vishwamitra 157
Vojta, M. 57

Wagle, G. S. 152
White, Justice 162, 164
Wilkinson, Thomas O. 113
Williams, Sir Glanville 31–2

Index of Subjects

Abortion
  definition 21
  legal status in various countries 119
  primitive methods 56
Abortion Act 53
Acharyas 40
Afghanistan 45
Ahimsa 34
Algeria 45
American Baptist Convention 39
American Law Institute 39
Amindivi 99, 144
Amrit Bazar Patrika 159
Andaman 98, 144
Andhra Pradesh 94, 144
Arabs 47
Argentina 55

Assam 94, 144
Assyrian code 22
Assyrians 24
Ashtanga Samgraha 42
Atharva-Veda 40–1
Atman 32
Ayuh 41
Ayurveda 41

Babylonians 24
Bangalore City 61
Bangla Desh 45
BCG vaccination 71
Belgium 55
Bhagavad-Gītā 35
Bhruna-hatya 44
Bihar 94, 144
Blastocyst 32

INDEX OF SUBJECTS

Bombay 61
Bourne v. *the Crown* 52
Brahman 32
Brihadyogatarangini 23
British Council of Churches 48
British Parliament 53
Buddhism 34
Buddhists 145

Calcutta 63
Calatropis gigantea 56
California 53
Canada 55
Catholic Church 49
   and war 33–4
   theology 35–6
Catholicism 26–8
Casti Connubi 27
Central Family Planning Board 83, 128
Central Family Planning Council 86
Chandigarh 98
Charaka Samhita 42
Chien Chin Fang 24
Child Marriage Restraint Act 70
Chile 55
China, People's Republic of 50, 55, 74
Christian Church 34
Christian era 22
Christians 145
Church of England 39
Colorado 53
Colombo Plan 71
Commonwealth 50
Communism 49
Cro-Magnon man 68

Dadra 98, 144
Dais 65
D and C 56, 58
Daman 99, 144
DDT 71
Delhi 61, 64, 98, 144
Delhi Demographic Research Centre 64
Demographic Training and Research Centre, Bombay 63
Denmark 50
Dharma Sutras 44
Diseases, Medical indication for induced abortion 120–7
District of Columbia 165
Diu 99, 144
DNA 30–1

Doe v. *Bolton* 161

Eastern Economist 154
Ebers Papyrus 22
Egypt 22
Embryo 32
Eugenics Protection Law 53, 109, 110
Exodus, Book of 23

Family Life Education 86
Family Planning Board 84
Family Planning Training and Research Centre, Bombay 63
Fatwah 48
Fertility 42
Fiqh 47
Finland 48
Foetus 21, 27, 32
France 26, 55

Gandhians 33
Gandhigram 61
Garbha-hatya 44
Garbapatana 44
Genesis, Book of 25
Georgia 161–4
German Democratic Republic 110
Germany, Federal Republic of (West Germany) 55
Goa 99, 144
Great Britain 45, 50, 51, 55, 66
Greeks 24
Gujarat 94, 144

Hallford 161
Hammurabic Code 22
Hanafy School of Law 47
Haryana 94, 144
Himachal Pradesh 99, 144
Hindus 24, 28, 32, 40, 45, 145
Hindu Code 22
Hinduism 34
Hindustan Latex Ltd 77
Humanae Vitae 27
Hungary 55
   abortions 113–15
   births 115
Hysterectomy 58

Incest 40, 42
India
   All India Radio 75
   birth and death rates 72–3
   census, 1951 144

INDEX OF SUBJECTS

census, 1961 144
census, 1971 144
expectation of life at birth 72
Family planning clinics 77
film industry 76
food consumption 75
growth rates 23
indigenous medical system 78
IUD 76-7
land area 74
malaria control 71
marriages 70
medical colleges 71
national income 74
panchayats 75
per capita income 74
Planning Commission 72, 84
political stability 72
population growth 69
population increase since freedom 70
Red Triangle 75
religious composition 145
tubectomy 76
under-enumeration of population 73
vasectomy 76
widow remarriage 71
Indian Lunacy Act, 1962 90
Indian Majority Act, 1875 90
Indian Medical Association 152
Indian Medical Council Act, 1956 85, 87
Indian Penal Code 66, 67, 90, 92, 104
Indian Penal Code Amendment Act XLII, 1949 78
Infant Life Preservation Act 51
Infanticide 47
Iran 45
Italy 55

Jainism 34, 145
Jammu 94, 144
Japan 55
  abortions 111-12
  sterilizations 113
Jews 25, 47
Journal of the Christian Medical Association of India 146
Judaism 25

Kahun Papyrus 22
Karma 32
Kashmir 94, 144
Kathaka Samhita 44

Kerala 94, 144
Khanna District 60
Koran 46, 48

Laccadive 99, 144
Lady Hardinge Medical College 64
Lambeth Conference 37-8
Latin America 65
Lok Sabha 90, 103

Madhya Pradesh 94, 144
Madras State (Tamil Nadu) 61, 144
Madurai District 61
Mahabharata 44
Maharashtra State 61
Malaysia 45
Malthusianism 49, 68
Manipur 99, 144
Marxism 49, 50
Medical Termination of Pregnancy Act, 1971 103, 106
Medical Termination of Pregnancy Bill 88
Meiosis 28
Menopause 42
Menstruation 42
Mexico 55
Minicoy 99, 144
Mississippi 53
Model Penal Code 39
Morocco 45
Moscow State University 57
Muftis 46
Muslims 45-7, 145
Mysore 60, 94, 144

Nagaland 97, 144
Nagar Haveli 98, 144
Nagpur Times 157
National Council of Churches 39
North East Frontier Agency 100, 144
New Delhi 64
New York City 166
New York State 166
Nicobar 98, 144
North Carolina 53
Norway 50

Offences Against the Person Act 51
Old Testament 22-3
Orissa 95, 144

Pakistan 45, 48
Persian Code 22
Planning Commission 72, 84

183

INDEX OF SUBJECTS

Poland 50
Pondicherry 100, 146
Poona 61
Portugal 26
Prana 32
Protestants 37–40
Puberty 42
Punjab 60–1, 95, 144

Quakers 33

Rajasthan 97, 144
Rajya Sabha 88, 90, 103
Ramayana 44
Rape 40
R. G. Kar Medical College 63
Rig-Veda 40
Roe et al. v. *Wade* 161
Roman Catholicism *see* Catholicism
Romans 24

Sāma-Veda 40
Samuels v. *Mackell* 162
Sarada Act 70
Scandinavia 50
Second World War 110, 113
Shariat 47
Sikhs 145
Sikkim 144
Smritis 44
Soviet Union 49, 50, 53, 57, 58, 96
Spain 26
Sterility 42
Suction pump, *see* vacuum aspirator
Sumerian Code 22
Sunnah 48
Supreme Court, US 161, 165, 167
Susruta Samhita 42
Sweden 50

Taittreya Aranyaka 44
Talmud 23
Tamil Nadu (Madras State) 61, 97, 144
Texas 164–5
The Pioneer 151
The Searchlight 152
Times of India 146
Tribune 156
Tripura 144
Tubectomy 27

Ulamas 46
Ulan Bator 50
Union Territories 93–4
Unitarian Universalist Association 40
United Arab Republic 45
United Nations 60
United Presbyterian Church 40
United States of America 39, 53–5, 70, 111
Upanga 41
Upanishads 23
Uruguay 55
Uttar Pradesh 97, 144

Vacuum aspirator 57–8
Vaidya Jeevanam 45
Vasectomy 27
Vatican 27
Vishnu Smriti 44

West Bengal 97, 144
World Health Organization 21, 71, 119
World population growth 68

Yagnavalkya Smriti 44
Yajur-Veda 40

Zygote 28, 30, 32

HQ766.5 .I5C43 1974

a742900000001014c

WITHDRAWN
From Bertrand Library

DATE DUE

DEC 11 1974	NOV 21 1977
FEB 3 1975	MAY 13 1978
FEB 19 1975	NOV 10 1979
FEB 25 1975	DEC 2 1981
	DEC 28 1981
DEC 26 1975	DEC 19 1981
MAY 24 1976	MAY 1 1983
MAY 10 1976	FEB 24 1984
DEC 6 1976	MAR 17 1985
	APR 26 1986
NOV 22 1976	MAY
1976	MAY 27 1986
MAY 18 1977	MAR 21 1988
MAY 9 1977	APR 29 '88
NOV 14 1977	MAY 9 '89
GAYLORD	MAR 17 1992